FISH VEGETABLE CHEESE AND CHICKEN COOKBOOK

Demiveg Excellence

FISH VEGETABLE CHEESE AND CHICKEN COOKBOOK

Demiveg Excellence

DAVID SCOTT

BLOOMSBURY

First published in Great Britain 1988
Copyright © 1988 by David Scott

Bloomsbury Publishing Ltd, 2 Soho Square, London W1V 5DE

ISBN 0−7475−0222−6

Designed by Fielding Rowinski
Photography by Chris Crofton
Food prepared by Carole Handslip
Styled by Maria Kelly
Phototypeset by Bookworm Typesetting, Manchester, England
Printed and bound in Great Britain by Butler & Tanner Ltd, Frome, Somerset

CONTENTS

Author's Note 7

Introduction and Basic Recipes 9

Soups 19

Starters 33

Salads 45

Vegetables 57

Cheese, Yoghurt and Cream 81

Fish and Shellfish 105

Chicken 137

Fruit Desserts 161

Conversion Tables 171

Oven Temperatures 171

British and American Equivalents 172

Index 173

ACKNOWLEDGEMENTS

Thanks for their help and advice to Brian Eames, Paula Williams and their colleagues at the Sea Fish Industry Authority; Susan Bush and Susan Hayes of the National Dairy Council; and Jane Beechey, Jo Beagan and Lindsay Morgan of the Fresh Fruit and Vegetable Information Bureau and the British Chicken Information Service.

AUTHOR'S NOTE

Most of the recipes and much of the accompanying information included in this book were provided by the Sea Fish Industry Authority, the National Dairy Council, the Fresh Fruit and Vegetable Information Bureau and the British Chicken Information Service. This came about in the following way. In the course of researching material for my previous book on demivegetarian food – *The Demiveg Cookbook* (Bloomsbury, 1987) – I approached each organization for help. The information they separately provided on that occasion was so good I subsequently decided to ask them if they would collaborate with me on a new demivegetarian cookery book. Happily they all agreed.

The four organizations have provided the basic nutritional, product and culinary information, which I have edited, and I have selected from their well-tasted collections of recipes those that suit the demivegetarian concept. I have also added some material and recipes of my own. (It should be noted that the ideas in this book are not necessarily those of the generic bodies.) Bloomsbury took the manuscript, added the beautiful colour pictures, and have designed and produced a book that is a pleasure to use.

INTRODUCTION
AND
BASIC RECIPES

The word 'demiveg' describes a way of eating that involves excluding all red meat from our diet and reducing the amount of foods high in fat, salt and sugar, while increasing the amount of vegetables, fish, chicken, dairy produce and fruit. It is a way of improving our diet and health without having to become completely vegetarian or be characterized as food faddists or increase the amount we spend on food. Demivegetarian is a sensible diet which leaves room for the occasional indulgence of perhaps more cream than we really need or some other treat we sometimes have the urge for. The premise of this book is that the touchstones of a good diet are moderation, awareness of our body's needs and a balance which can, if we wish, now and again swing from austerity to luxury.

The recipes are divided into the following chapters: Basic Recipes; Soups; Starters; Salads; Vegetables; Fish and Shellfish; Chicken; Cheese, Yoghurt and Cream; and Fruit Desserts. Grains and legume dishes do not appear as separate chapters but grains and beans are included as ingredients or accompaniments in a variety of recipes across a range of chapters.

The essence of a demivegetarian diet is that it combines different foodstuffs; thus, small amounts of fish or chicken may, for instance, appear in vegetable recipes, just as vegetables can be an important ingredient in, say, a cheese-based dish. I have selected recipes that make tasty, uncomplicated but colourful dishes and provide an enjoyable, healthy, energy-giving and nutritionally balanced diet.

Demiveg and Nutrition

The combination of foods we eat and their quantity, both on their own and in relation to one another, are important in a good demivegetarian diet. We need to ensure that we eat satisfactory amounts of protein, carbohydrates, vitamins, minerals, fibre and fat, and that we maintain a balance between what we eat and the energy we expend. Otherwise we get too thin or too fat. While grains, as found in wholemeal bread and pasta, brown rice and unrefined breakfast cereals, eaten in combination with fresh and cooked vegetables and fruit are an important part of a balanced diet, if, alongside these two food groups, we also eat chicken, fish, eggs, milk, yoghurt and cheese, our diet will contain all the nutrients we require in satisfactory quantities and in the right combinations, and at the same time will be low in amount of fat it contains.

Individual Nutrients

PROTEIN

It used to be thought that without a 'good helping' of meat we would not get sufficient protein, but the truth is that most of us eat more protein than we need — the excess is used as an energy source or simply goes to fat. We can comfortably get all the protein we need from dairy products, eggs, fish and poultry and a variety of foods which include cereals, nuts, beans and seeds. Remember also that it is important to combine foods from different food groups at the same meal. In this way we get the best nutritional protein value from them.

IRON

Most of the nutrients that meat provides can be obtained from other foods, with perhaps the exception of iron. Iron is needed to make sufficient haemoglobin, which is the oxygen-carrying protein present in red blood cells. If we do not have enough of this we become anaemic. The iron from meat, including poultry, is better absorbed than the iron from other foods, but as the body gets used to eating less meat, it becomes more efficient at absorbing iron from foods like bread and flour, green vegetables, eggs and pulse vegetables. The absorption is facilitated if a good source of vitamin C is eaten at the same time – for example, include a salad and/or fresh fruit and/or green vegetables in each meal.

CALCIUM

Calcium is needed for the growth and maintenance of bones and teeth. In a normal diet we get most of our intake from milk (skimmed or whole), milk products and cheese, and because of our consumption of these products calcium deficiency is rare. However, growing children, expectant or nursing mothers and the elderly, who need more than the average amount of calcium, should ensure a healthy supply of calcium-containing foods in their diets. Sources besides dairy produce are tinned fish, bread with calcium added and, for vegans, tofu or beancurd.

SALT

Salt (sodium chloride) is found naturally in a wide variety of foods and is an essential compound in the body. However, over the years, people have acquired a taste for a much higher level of salt than is probably good for them.

If you like a lot of salt on your food or enjoy salty foods, try to cut down on them. As a substitute you could experiment with herbs and other flavourings, such as peppers and spices. If you are extremely active or live in a hot humid climate you will need to increase your salt intake because salt is lost in perspiration.

SUGAR

Sugar is often thought to be essential in providing us with energy, but in fact we can obtain all the energy we need from other foods. Sugar provides only calories and contains no vitamins, minerals or protein, and it displaces other, more nutritious, foods from our diet.

Most of us, however, developed a liking for sweet things in childhood and this tends to stay with us throughout our lives. Thus we need to exercise some control over the amount of cakes, chocolate and puddings we eat and gradually to wean ourselves off adding spoonfuls of sugar to tea, coffee and breakfast cereal, and to choose cereals which have no added sugar.

Demiveg and Fresh Foods

Fresh foods are most important in a demiveg diet because they are highly nutritious. Whenever possible, buy fresh fruit and vegetables and fresh fish in season, when they are at their tastiest and cheapest. Convenience foods can help to give variety to our meals, but those which are highly salted or coloured or have added sugar or are high in fat should be avoided. Tinned vegetables are fine if you are in a hurry, but the canning process can alter their vitamin content and the vegetables are often canned in a very salty solution. Therefore they should only be used now and again.

Tinned fruit is usually canned in a heavy syrup, so it too should be avoided. Try to use fruit which is tinned in pure fruit juice. Fresh fruit, like fresh vegetables, generally has a far better flavour and texture than the tinned variety.

Frozen vegetables are often satisfactory, but they often lose their fresh flavour and texture during freezing or defrosting. They are usually more expensive than fresh items. Fresh vegetables should be cooked in the minimum amount of fast-boiling water for as short a time as possible in order to retain the maximum level of vitamins.

Demiveg and Exercise

For a healthy way of life, eating and exercise go together. Regular exercise every day, be it walking, cycling, swimming, dancing or whatever you most enjoy, is a good habit to develop.

Suggestions for Following a Healthy Demiveg Diet

Eat lots of vegetables and fresh fruit each day. Include at least one salad a day with your meals.

Ensure whole grains in the form of wholemeal bread, wholemeal pasta, brown rice or other cooked grains and breakfast cereals form part of your staple diet.

Substitute poultry or fish for red meat. Eat fish and chicken at least twice a week but not necessarily always as a main meal.

Use semi-skimmed or skimmed milk and take advantage of low-fat dairy products (yoghurt and hard and soft cheeses); eat butter only moderately; for cooking and dressings use vegetable oils such as olive oil, sunflower oil and corn oil. Remember, however, to eat only moderate amounts of any fats and oils.

Eat a wide selection of different foods.

Buy good-quality provisions and, where appropriate, buy them when in season. Some fish are seasonal and can then be particularly inexpensive, such as sprats.

Buy the freshest fish you can find. Frozen fish, well kept in undamaged packaging, is a good alternative.

Always dilute fruit juice. The neat variety from the carton is too concentrated for most people to digest easily.

Avoid too many processed foods.

Avoid foods that contain a lot of artificial flavourings and colourings.

Avoid overcooking vegetables and fish.

Avoid too many snacks such as biscuits, cakes, pastries, ice cream, roasted and salted peanuts, crisps.

Avoid sugared breakfast cereals, soft drinks and squashes, chocolates and other sweets.

Avoid eating hardened margarines.

If as a general rule you follow the above suggestions, then there is no reason not occasionally to include in your diet refined foods such as white sugar, white rice and white bread and sometimes to eat butter and cream cakes – but, remember, moderation is the word. On that basis, if, for instance, you prefer white rice to brown rice, then eat white rice, but make sure you compensate for this by eating other whole grains, wholemeal bread and wholemeal pasta.

Note: More detailed nutritional information and advice on choosing, preparing and cooking fish, chicken, vegetables, fruit and dairy produce are given in the individual chapters.

BASIC RECIPES

This section contains basic recipes for ingredients such as chicken stock, fish stock, tomato sauce, French dressing and shortcrust pastry that are used in more than one recipe in the book.

Raw Tomato Sauce
Makes ½ pint (300 ml)

Use good, fresh, ripe tomatoes.

1 lb (450 g) ripe tomatoes, skinned and seeded
1 tablespoon wine vinegar
2 tablespoons olive oil
1 tablespoon finely chopped parsley
1 teaspoon dried oregano
salt and freshly ground black pepper to taste

Place all the ingredients in a liquidizer and blend at a low speed until a smooth sauce is obtained. Use the sauce over delicate vegetables, either as it is or thinned with whipping cream.

Note: For a very quick sauce use tinned tomatoes in place of the fresh ones.

Tomato Sauce
Makes about 1½ pints (850 ml)

2 oz (50 g) butter or vegetable oil
1 medium onion, finely diced
2 lb (900 g) tinned tomatoes, drained
4 cloves garlic, crushed
1 medium green pepper, seeded, cored and diced
2 teaspoons crushed oregano
2 tablespoons chopped fresh parsley
1 bay leaf
salt and freshly ground black pepper to taste

In a heavy saucepan melt the butter or warm the oil, and fry the onions over a low heat until soft. Chop the tomatoes into small pieces and add them, with the garlic and green pepper, to the onions. Stir well and simmer for 10 minutes. Add the herbs and season with salt and black pepper. Simmer for a further 10 minutes. Use immediately or allow to cool.

For a thicker tomato sauce suitable for some types of pizza or for use with stuffings for vegetable and pasta dishes, add 6 oz (175 g) tomato purée with the chopped tomatoes.

Basic Mayonnaise

Makes about ½ pint (300 ml)

1 large egg
1 teaspoon prepared mustard
a good pinch salt
9 fl oz (250 ml) vegetable oil
wine vinegar (up to 2 tablespoons)
additional salt and freshly ground black pepper to taste

Break the egg into a bowl or liquidizer goblet, add the mustard and salt. Beat or blend at medium speed until the mixture thickens slightly. Still beating, pour in the oil from a measuring jug, drop by drop initially and then, as the mixture begins to thicken, in a slow but steady stream until all the oil is absorbed. Carefully beat or blend in the wine vinegar and season with more salt and pepper. Store in a cool place. Mayonnaise will not keep for much longer than a day.

Chicken Stock

Makes 5 pints (3 litres)

Chicken stock takes some time to make and requires a whole chicken; hence it is worth preparing a decent amount at a time. Use the leftover cooked chicken in salads, curries, pilavs or other chicken dishes.

3 – 4 lb (1 – 1.2 kg) medium-quality chicken, quartered
7 pints (4 litres) water
1 large onion, quartered
2 large carrots, chopped
2 celery stalks, chopped
4 – 5 bay leaves
salt and freshly ground black pepper to taste

Put the chicken pieces and water into a large pot and bring to the boil. Skim off any froth that forms and add the other ingredients. Return to the boil, reduce the heat, cover and simmer for 2 hours or more. Strain off the stock. If some of the stock is required immediately, skim off the fat; otherwise let it cool and then refrigerate. Excess solidified fat may then be removed easily.

Fish stock

Makes 3¹/₄ pints (1.8 litres)

Fresh fish can be quite expensive, but fish stock, which is essential for making good fish soup, is actually made from scrap parts of fish – the head, tail and bones – which cost next to nothing. The best-tasting stock is made from the scraps of white flat fish such as sole, plaice, halibut and flounder.

2 lb (900 g) bones, heads and tails of sole or other fish, washed
1 large leek, chopped
1 large carrot, chopped
¹/₂ bunch parsley, chopped
2 sticks celery, chopped
juice of 1 lemon
4 pints (2.2 litres) water
salt and black pepper to taste

Put all the ingredients into a large pan and bring slowly to the boil. Reduce the heat and simmer, covered, for 1 hour. Occasionally remove the lid and skim off any scum that has formed. Strain off the stock. Use immediately or refrigerate or deep-freeze. If refrigerated, it should be used within two to three days.

Quick Vegetable Stock

Makes 2 pints (1 litre)

This quick stock is handy to make if you have a food processor so you can chop the vegetables speedily. Root vegetables other than those given in the recipe may be used.

2¹/₂ pints (1.4 litres) water
2 medium onions
1 medium potato
1 medium carrot or parsnip
1 leek
2 sticks celery
2 tomatoes
2 cloves garlic
chopped parsley or other fresh herbs as available
salt and freshly ground black pepper to taste

Put the water into a large pan and bring to the boil. Meanwhile finely chop the vegetables and garlic by hand or in a food processor. Put them into the pan and add the other ingredients. Return to the boil, reduce heat, cover and gently boil for 20–25 minutes. Strain the stock and gently press the vegetables to extract as much liquid as possible. Discard the vegetables. The stock is ready to use, and can be either chilled or frozen. If chilled it should be used within three days.

Wholewheat Shortcrust Pastry
Makes 10 oz (275 g)

3 oz (75 g) plain flour and 3 oz (75 g)
wholewheat flour or 6 oz (150 g) wholewheat flour
¼ teaspoon salt
3½ oz (90 g) butter or vegetable margarine
iced water

Mix the flour and salt together in a bowl. Rub in the butter or margarine until the mixture resembles breadcrumbs. Add enough water to form a dough (about 2 fl oz or 50 ml). If not using immediately, cover the pastry with a damp cloth and store it in the refrigerator.

Fila Pastry

Fila pastry (also called filo or phyllo or by its Arabic name *ajeen*) is a delicate paper-thin pastry. It is very versatile and most useful to the pastry cook. The paper-thin sheets of pastry can be used singly or built up into layers to any thickness. They are also flexible and can be rolled or folded into a wide variety of shapes. In the Middle East, where it is very popular, fila pastry is used to make many different pastries in all shapes and sizes with a variety of fillings.

Making fila pastry at home requires a lot of skill, patience and time; nowadays it is normally bought ready prepared. It is readily available in good delicatessens and most Greek food stores. It is normally sold in standard-size packs of 1 lb (450 g) or 8 oz (225 g) containing about 24 or 12 sheets respectively. Each leaf of pastry is usually 20 × 12 in (50 × 30 cm) in size. Commercially produced fila keeps for weeks under refrigeration, but once a pack has been opened or the pastry has been exposed to the heat of the kitchen the sheets start to dry out and crumble.

To use fila pastry, remove from the wrap only as many sheets as you intend to use immediately. Store the unwrapped sheets between two dry teatowels and drape a third dampened teatowel over the top. Remove the individual sheets of pastry from under the teatowels as required and brush them sparsely with melted butter to retain their flexibility. Do not worry if sheets tear while you are using them because you can repair or re-cover them with another sheet.

Basic French Dressing
Makes 7 fl oz (200 ml)

¹/₄ pint (150 ml) olive oil
³/₄ teaspoon salt
pinch freshly ground black pepper
3 tablespoons vinegar, wine vinegar or lemon juice

Shake all the ingredients in a jar or combine them in a blender for a few seconds.

VARIATIONS
Add all or any one of the following:

¹/₂ teaspoon dry mustard
¹/₂ teaspoon paprika
1 crushed clove of garlic
1 tablespoon minced onion

SOUPS

Soups are an important part of a demivegetarian diet as they combine a wide variety of ingredients from the main demivegetarian food groups. Vegetables, beans, grains, fish, chicken, milk, cheese, yoghurt and even fruit are all used, either individually or in combination, to make the soups given here. Quite a few of the recipes require stock. For this you can use your own stock recipe or one of those given on pp. '15–16 or stock cubes. Sometimes water can be used instead of stock, in which case, towards the end of the cooking time you should blend some of the soup to give texture and flavour to the liquid. This technique usually works well with soups containing root vegetables.

The appearance of a soup is improved by garnishing, but often the garnish turns out to be parsley or watercress. I normally prefer the garnish to reflect one of the ingredients in the soup and I have put this idea into practice in some of the recipes given here. Thus, if a soup contains celery, reserve a few celery leaves for garnish; if it contains almonds, garnish with toasted almonds.

FISH SOUPS

Italian Fish and Mussel Stew
Serves 4

Use any filleted white fish in this recipe. Serve the stew with brown bread or rice for a light meal or it can be eaten on its own as a substantial first course.

2 teaspoons olive oil
1 medium onion, sliced
1 clove garlic, crushed
8 oz (225 g) carrots, chopped
14 oz (400 g) tin tomatoes
12 black olives, stoned
1 bay leaf
8 fl oz (225 ml) water or stock
salt and freshly ground black pepper to taste
1 lb (450 g) white fish, skinned, filleted and cubed
12 fresh mussels in their shells, cleaned and scraped
freshly chopped parsley or fresh basil to garnish

Heat the oil in a saucepan and add the onion, garlic and carrots. Fry until the onion is softened. Add the tomatoes, olives, bay leaf, water or stock, salt and black pepper and the fish. Simmer for 8–10 minutes. Add the mussels and simmer for a further 5–6 minutes or until the shells open. Adjust the seasoning and serve garnished with parsley or basil.

Note: Add more or less water or stock for a thinner or richer stew.

Herring and Vegetable Soup
Serves 6

Herring is flavoursome, readily available and economical to buy and makes an excellent ingredient in soup. This soup is tasty and nutritious. For the very best flavour make it the day before, refrigerate overnight and reheat when needed.

2 pints (1.1 litres) fish or chicken stock
8 oz (225 g) carrots, diced (reserve a few thin slices for garnish)
8 oz (225 g) swede, diced
1 lb (450 g) herring fillets, diced
2 teaspoons tomato purée
salt and freshly ground black pepper to taste

Put the stock into a large saucepan. Add the carrots and swede and cook until tender. Add the diced fillets of fish and cook gently for 5 minutes. Allow to cool slightly. Add the tomato purée and season with salt and black pepper. Liquidize or place in a food processor and blend for 3–4 minutes until smooth. Return the liquid to the pan and heat it until it just begins to simmer. Serve garnished with carrot slices.

Haddock or Coley and Sweetcorn Soup
Serves 6

Haddock is at its best from September to February, but is available all year round; coley is available all year round and makes a good economic alternative. For a filling, everyday soup use coley; for a special occasion use haddock or cod. Use the bones and head of the fish to make stock.

4 sticks celery, chopped (reserve a few leaves for garnish)
1 pint (550 ml) fish or chicken stock
½ pint (275 ml) skimmed or semi-skimmed milk
1½ lb (675 g) coley, haddock or cod fillets, skinned and cubed
10 oz (275 g) sweetcorn (if using tinned corn, it should be drained)
salt and freshly ground black pepper to taste
2 tablespoons cornflour

Simmer the celery in the stock until just tender. Add the milk, fish, sweetcorn, salt and black pepper. Simmer gently taking care not to allow the soup to boil, for 8–10 minutes or until the fish is tender. Blend the cornflour with a little cold water and stir it into the soup. Simmer, stirring, until the soup has thickened. Serve garnished with celery leaves.

Paddy's Mussel, Potato and Apple Soup with Wine Stock
Serves 4

This is a recipe often cooked by my restaurant partner, Paddy Byrne.

2 pints (1 litre) mussels
1 lb (450 g) potatoes, peeled and diced
1 Granny Smith apple, cored and diced
2 cloves garlic, peeled and chopped
4 tablespoons chopped parsley
1½ oz (40 g) butter
5 oz (125 g) single cream
3 egg yolks
salt and freshly ground black pepper to taste

WINE STOCK
1 pint (1½ litres) water
½ bottle dry white wine
1 medium onion, peeled
3 cloves
2 medium carrots
1 leek
1 stick celery
a few parsley stalks
½ teaspoon whole black peppercorns
½ teaspoon whole white peppercorns
thick slice of lemon
sprig of thyme

Begin by making the stock. Stud the onion with the cloves, and roughly slice the carrots, leek and celery. Place all the ingredients in a saucepan, bring the contents to a vigorous boil and maintain for a couple of minutes, then reduce the heat, loosely cover the pan and let the stock bubble gently for 30 minutes. Strain and set aside.

While waiting for the stock to cook, clean and de-beard the mussels, place them in a large pan and cook over a high heat, shaking repeatedly for three minutes or until all the mussels are open. Strain the mussels, reserving the liquid, and remove and set aside the meat.

To make the soup, first melt the butter in a clean pan, add the garlic and cook briefly. Then add the potato and apple and a little salt. Add the mussel liquor (taking care to leave any sand behind) and 1½ pints (800 ml) of the prepared stock and bring to the boil. Reduce the heat, cover and cook for 30 minutes or until the potato is cooked. Add the mussel meat and cook for a further three minutes. Now reduce the heat to a minimum and stir in the parsley. In a small bowl, mix the egg yolks with the cream and beat in a ladleful of liquid from the pan. Return this mixture to the pan, stirring briefly while the soup thickens. Taste and adjust the seasoning.

Prawn and Ginger Soup
Serves 4

This simple but delicious Indonesian soup is best made with fresh prawns, although frozen prawns can be used successfully. To prepare fresh prawns, remove the head, tail, legs and shell and, if the prawns are large, remove the vein along the back with a sharp knife. You can use the discarded parts of the prawns to make a stock. This soup can also be made with coconut milk – see the variation below.

2 tablespoons vegetable oil
2 cloves garlic, crushed
1/2 in (1 cm) root ginger, finely chopped
2 small onions, finely sliced
1/2 teaspoon ground coriander
6 oz (175 g) fresh or frozen prawns, peeled and cleaned
1 pint (550 ml) water or stock
salt and freshly ground black pepper to taste
4 oz (100 g) Chinese egg noodles
1 small leek, thinly sliced

Heat the oil in a heavy pan, add the garlic, ginger and onions and sauté, stirring, until the onion is softened. Add the coriander and prawns and cook, stirring, for 2–3 minutes. Add the water or stock and season with salt and black pepper. Bring to the boil, reduce the heat and simmer for 15 minutes. Add the noodles, stir well and simmer for a further 8 minutes. Add the leek, adjust the seasoning and cook the soup gently for another 5 minutes.

VARIATION

Tinned coconut milk can be substituted for half the stock or water. Follow the same procedure as given in the recipe, but after adding the water or stock and coconut milk mixture to the prawns, stir the soup continuously until it comes to the boil and then only allow it to simmer very gently. This prevents the coconut milk from curdling.

CHILLED SOUPS

Chilled soup is delicious on a warm evening; on cooler nights it can be served as a refreshing starter to a hot main dish. Remember, however, that a chilled soup needs to be more highly flavoured than a hot one. In the following three recipes one soup is liberally flavoured with spices, another with fresh herbs, and the third, a fruit soup, with wine.

Chilled Fresh Tomato and Herb Soup
Serves 6

1½ lb (900 g) ripe tomatoes
½ cucumber, roughly chopped
1 red pepper, roughly chopped
4 spring onions, roughly chopped
2 cloves garlic, peeled
juice of ½ small lemon
1 oz (25 g) fresh breadcrumbs
4 tablespoons olive oil
2 tablespoons freshly chopped parsley
2 tablespoons freshly chopped chervil
1 tablespoon freshly chopped tarragon
12 coriander seeds, well crushed
salt and freshly ground black pepper to taste

GARNISH
Select two or three from the following:

diced cucumber
diced red and green peppers
finely sliced celery
pitted black olives
roasted almonds

Cut the tomatoes in half horizontally and squeeze them lightly to expel the seeds and excess moisture. Then chop them roughly and place the chopped flesh in a liquidizer and blend until barely smooth. Pour the puréed tomatoes into a mixing bowl and set aside. Place the cucumber, red pepper, spring onions, garlic, lemon juice, breadcrumbs and olive oil in the liquidizer and blend until smooth. Add this mixture to the tomato purée, stir in the freshly chopped herbs and the crushed coriander seeds and season with black pepper and salt. Pour the soup into a serving bowl and set aside to chill. Just before serving add three or four ice cubes. Let each person garnish his or her own soup.

For a lighter soup use only 1 lb (450 g) tomatoes and blend with them ½ pint (300 ml) cold water.

A chilled tureen of smooth gazpacho-style soup surrounded by small bowls containing chopped vegetables makes a splendid centrepiece for an informal meal. The soup can be prepared swiftly in a liquidizer, but it does need to be made at least an hour ahead of serving to give it time to chill and to allow the flavours to mingle. Other fresh herbs may be substituted for the parsley, chervil and tarragon.

Curried Apple Soup
Serves 4

½ oz (15 g) butter
1 medium onion, finely chopped
1 lb (450 g) dessert apples, peeled, cored and chopped
½–1 tablespoon medium curry powder
1 pint (550 ml) chicken stock
cinnamon stick (optional)
8 fl oz (225 ml) skimmed milk
5 oz (150 g) natural yoghurt
1 dessert apple to garnish

Melt the butter in a large saucepan, add the onion and apple. Cover and cook gently until the apples and onion are tender. Add the curry powder and cook over a medium heat, stirring, for 2–3 minutes. Add the stock and cinnamon if used. Bring to the boil, cover and simmer for 10 minutes, stirring occasionally. Allow to cool, then purée the soup in a blender. Stir in the milk and yoghurt. Cover and chill for 2 hours. Just before serving, stir the soup well and pour it into a serving dish or dishes. Garnish with finely chopped or sliced apple, which should be prepared as soon before serving as possible and tossed in lemon juice to prevent discoloration.

Peach, Almond and Wine Soup
Serves 4

3 large ripe peaches
juice of 1/2 lemon
3 oz (75 g) blanched almonds
3/4 pint (450 ml) dry white wine
2 egg yolks
1 tablespoon chopped fresh tarragon
1/4 pint (150 ml) single cream
4 sprigs tarragon to garnish

Make a nick in the skin at the stalk end of each peach, plunge the peaches into a bowl of boiling water for 45 seconds, remove them with a slotted spoon and slide off the skins. Halve and stone the peaches and chop the flesh. Put the peach flesh into a liquidizer with the lemon juice, almonds, white wine, egg yolks and chopped tarragon and blend until smooth. Stir in the cream. Chill the soup thoroughly. To serve, pour the soup into four small glass bowls. Add an ice cube or two to each one and garnish with a sprig of tarragon.

WINTER VEGETABLE SOUPS

The advantages of root vegetable soups are that they do not need a stock and that a filling and tasty soup can be made quickly from scratch. The first recipe was given to me by the Fresh Fruit and Vegetable Information Bureau and the following one by my restaurant partner, Paddy Byrne.

Spicy Root Vegetable Soup
Serves 4

1 medium onion, peeled and finely chopped
1 tablespoon olive oil
1 clove garlic, crushed
1/4 teaspoon chilli powder
1/4 teaspoon ground ginger
1/4 teaspoon ground cumin
1/4 teaspoon ground nutmeg
1 tablespoon flour
1 1/2 pints (750 ml) water
2 small parsnips, peeled and diced
1 medium turnip, peeled and diced
1 swede, peeled and diced
salt and freshly ground black pepper to taste

Fry the onion in the oil together with the garlic, chilli powder, ginger, cumin and nutmeg for 2–3 minutes until the onion is soft. Stir in the flour and cook for 30 seconds. Gradually add the water, stirring continuously. Add the root vegetables and season with salt and black pepper. Cover the pan and simmer for 20 minutes until the vegetables are just tender. Stir the soup with a wooden spoon or, if you prefer, blend it in a liquidizer until it has the required texture.

Potato and Carrot Soup

Serves 4

1 oz (25 g) butter
8 oz (225 g) onions, thinly sliced
8 oz (225 g) carrots, thinly sliced
1 stick celery, thinly sliced (optional)
1 small white turnip, thinly sliced (optional)
1 lb (450 g) potatoes, peeled and cut into small dice
bouquet garni (parsley stalks, bay leaf, sprig of thyme)
salt and freshly ground black pepper to taste

Melt the butter in a pan, add the sliced onions and cook them uncovered over a low heat until they are quite soft. Add the carrots and the celery and turnip if used. Stir well and cook them with the onions for 1–2 minutes. Add the diced potatoes, stir these into the other vegetables and then add enough water to cover the vegetables by about ½ in (1 cm). Add the bouquet garni and salt, cover and turn up the heat. Once the soup is boiling, reduce the heat to a slow simmer and cook for 20 minutes or until the vegetables are soft. Add the black pepper, adjust the salt and remove the herbs. Allow the soup to cool slightly, then either beat it with a wooden spoon or blend it in a liquidizer.

Butterbean Soup
Serves 4–6

Dried beans or pulses are a convenient soup ingredient. They are always available in the store cupboard and they add flavour, body and nutrients to any soup. Their only drawback is that they have to be soaked overnight before use. Nowadays red beans or chickpeas are very popular, but old standbys such as butter beans should not be forgotten.

4 oz (100 g) butter beans
1 pint (550 ml) water
2 sticks celery, chopped
2 large carrots, peeled and sliced
2 small leeks, washed and sliced
1 medium onion, chopped
¼ level teaspoon dried thyme
pinch cayenne pepper
1 bay leaf
salt and freshly ground black pepper to taste
½ pint (275 ml) fresh whole or skimmed milk
2 fl oz (50 ml) natural yoghurt or sour cream

Place the beans and water in a saucepan and bring them to the boil. Remove the pan from the heat. Pour the contents into a bowl, cover and leave the beans to soak overnight. The next day drain the beans, put them in a saucepan with 1 pint (550 ml) fresh water and bring them to the boil. Add the celery, carrot, leeks, onion, thyme, cayenne pepper and bay leaf. Cover and simmer for 45 minutes or until the beans are tender. Allow to cool. Blend the soup until smooth, then return it to the rinsed saucepan. Season with salt and black pepper, and then add the milk. Reheat the soup to boiling point and stir in the yoghurt or sour cream.

Potato and Broccoli Soup
Serves 4

Winter greens and root vegetables make a nutritious combination and provide the vitamins and minerals we need during the cold, sunless months. This soup simply uses two of the vegetables most readily available.

1 small onion, finely chopped
1 oz (25 g) butter
1 lb (450 g) potatoes, peeled and cut into ¾ in (2 cm) cubes
1 oz (25 g) wholemeal flour
1 pint (550 ml) chicken or vegetable stock or water
½ pint (275 ml) fresh or skimmed milk
salt and freshly ground black pepper to taste
6 oz (175 g) broccoli, divided into small florets

Fry the onion gently in the butter for 3 minutes. Add the cubed potatoes and fry them with the onion for a further minute. Stir in the flour and cook for 30 seconds. Gradually stir in the stock or water and the milk and bring to the boil. Add the seasoning and simmer for 10–15 minutes (20 minutes if you are using water instead of stock). If you are using water, stir the soup well with a wooden spoon to break up the potato and add to the flavour. Add the broccoli and simmer for a further 4–5 minutes until the vegetables are just tender. Serve.

Note: This gives a textured soup; for a smoother soup, allow the mixture to cool, then blend it in a liquidizer or food processor and reheat.

Cucumber and Chive Soup
Serves 4

This gently flavoured, refreshing soup can be served hot or cold.

1 small onion, finely chopped
½ cucumber, finely diced (reserve some for garnish)
1 oz (25 g) vegetable margarine or butter
1 oz (25 g) wholemeal flour
¾ pint (450 ml) chicken or vegetable stock
½ pint (275 ml) fresh or skimmed milk
2 tablespoons finely chopped fresh chives
salt and freshly ground black pepper to taste

In a pan fry the onion and cucumber in the margarine or butter until the onion is soft. Stir in the flour and cook for a further minute. Add the stock, milk and chives, and season with salt and black pepper. Simmer for about 15 minutes. Allow to cool, then blend the soup until it is almost smooth but still has some texture. Serve hot or cold and garnished with the reserved diced cucumber.

Tomato Soup with Cottage Cheese
Serves 4

Served with bread and a green salad, this soup provides a low-fat, nutritious light meal. Use yoghurt instead of cream for the garnish if you are trying to reduce your fat intake.

1 oz (25 g) butter
1 small onion, finely chopped
1 lb (450 g) tomatoes, washed and halved
½ pint (275 ml) chicken stock
2 tablespoons tomato purée
bouquet garni (parsley stalks, bay leaf, sprig of thyme)
4 oz (100 g) cottage cheese
salt and freshly ground black pepper to taste
fresh double cream or natural yoghurt

Melt the butter in a pan, add the onion and cook without browning for 5 minutes. Add the tomatoes, stock, tomato purée and bouquet garni. Cover and simmer for 15–20 minutes. Stir in the cottage cheese. Allow to cool, then liquidize the soup. Return it to the pan and season with salt and black pepper. Serve the soup piping hot and decorated with a swirl of cream or yoghurt.

Spicy Carrot and Orange Soup
Serves 4

This unusual combination of carrot, orange and ginger, can be served hot or well chilled.

1 oz (25 g) vegetable margarine or butter
1 lb (450 g) carrots, roughly chopped
1 medium onion, chopped
1 clove garlic, crushed
1 teaspoon grated root ginger or ¼ teaspoon ground ginger
1 pint (550 ml) chicken or vegetable stock
grated rind of ½ orange
juice of 2 oranges
salt and freshly ground black pepper to taste
1 egg yolk

Melt the margarine or butter in a saucepan and add the carrots and onion. Cook for 5 minutes and then add the garlic, ginger, stock, orange rind and juice. Bring to the boil, reduce the heat and simmer for 15 minutes or until the carrots are very tender. Blend the soup in a liquidizer until smooth, then return it to the pan. Reheat, season with salt and black pepper and gently whisk in the egg yolk. Serve hot or cold and garnished with a little grated orange zest.

Lettuce and Tarragon Soup
Serves 4

A good summer soup when lettuce is abundant, its light herb flavour suits the hoped-for warmth of the days.

½ large lettuce (iceberg, for example)
1 medium onion, finely chopped
2 oz (50 g) margarine or butter
1 clove garlic, crushed
1 oz (25 g) plain flour
1¼ pint (700 ml) chicken stock
1 tablespoon chopped fresh tarragon or 1 teaspoon dried tarragon
salt and freshly ground black pepper to taste
¼ pint (150 ml) thick natural yoghurt or sour cream
tarragon leaves to garnish

Shred the lettuce finely. Set aside 2–3 tablespoons of chopped centre leaves for garnish. Fry the onion gently in the margarine or butter for 3–4 minutes, add the garlic and flour and stir over the heat for 1 minute. Gradually stir in the stock and bring it to the boil. Add most of the shredded lettuce, the tarragon and salt and black pepper. Simmer for 20 minutes. Blend the soup in a liquidizer until smooth, return it to a clean pan and heat through. Add the yoghurt or sour cream and reserved shredded lettuce, and heat through again, stirring. Serve the soup piping hot and garnished with fresh tarragon and shredded lettuce.

Note: If using dried tarragon, garnish with watercress.

Celery and Almond Soup
Serves 4

Almonds are a good ingredient in soups. They have a nutty but sweet flavour, they blend well and they give a milky texture to the soup.

1 oz (25 g) vegetable margarine or butter
1 medium onion, chopped
¾ head celery, cleaned and chopped (reserve a few leaves for garnish)
1 bay leaf
1 medium potato, peeled and chopped
2 oz (50 g) blanched almonds, lightly dry-toasted (reserve a few for garnish)
1¼ pint (700 ml) chicken stock
salt and freshly ground black pepper to taste

To dry-toast the almonds, heat them in a small dry frying pan over a moderate heat until they are just starting to brown. Heat the margarine or butter in a saucepan and sauté the onion for 2−3 minutes until softened. Add the celery and sauté, stirring, for a further 3 minutes. Add the bay leaf, potato, almonds and stock, and season with salt and black pepper. Bring to the boil, cover, reduce the heat and simmer for 20−25 minutes. Remove the bay leaf, allow to cool, and then blend the soup until it is smooth. Return the soup to the rinsed pan and reheat. Serve garnished with celery leaves and almonds.

Spring Nettle Soup
Serves 4

Nettles are a perennial plant that can be cooked just like spinach. They are particularly good in the spring when the leaves are young and tender. Use the tops of the plants for the mildest flavour.

2 tablespoons vegetable oil
1 medium onion, chopped
1 small clove garlic, crushed
1 large potato, scrubbed and chopped
1 lb (450 g) young nettles
1¾ pints (1 litre) water
1 teaspoon lemon juice
½ teaspoon ground nutmeg
salt to taste

Heat the oil in a pan and sauté the onion and garlic for 5 minutes. Add the potato, nettles, water and lemon juice. Bring to the boil, reduce the heat, cover and cook for 20 minutes. Allow to cool. Liquidize the soup in a blender with the nutmeg and salt. Reheat and serve.

Lettuce and Tarragon Soup (page 31)

Welsh Cheese and Strawberry Filled Melon (page 39)

STARTERS

The type of starter you serve at the beginning of a meal should take into account the nature of the main course. Thus a fish main course is best preceded by a vegetable, chicken or dairy-produce starter rather than by another fish dish; a filling main meal requires a light, appetizing first course; while a robust starter can be followed by a light main dish. The recipes given here range from simple dips to more exotic hors d'oeuvre such as chicken parcels wrapped in nori seaweed. Many of them, made in large quantities, may also be served as main dishes and all of them are suitable for inclusion in a buffet meal.

YOGHURT DIPS

Dips are quick to prepare and, served with fresh seasonal vegetables cut into bite-size shapes (*crudités*), they make simple but delicious and refreshing starters. They are also ideal for a finger buffet. All the dips given here contain yoghurt as an ingredient. Yoghurt is versatile, good for the digestion and worthy of a regular place in our diets.

Beetroot Dip
Serves 4

8 oz (225 g) plain cottage cheese
1 tablespoon mayonnaise
5 fl oz (150 ml) natural yoghurt (or sour cream)
2 small cooked beetroots, grated

Sieve the cottage cheese into a bowl. Stir in the mayonnaise and yoghurt or soured cream. Just before serving stir in the beetroot.

Derby Dip
Serves 4

8 oz (225 g) plain cottage cheese
4 oz (100 g) Sage Derby cheese, grated
5 radishes
5 fl oz (150 ml) plain yoghurt

Sieve the cottage cheese into a bowl. Stir in 3 oz (75 g) of the Derby cheese. Finely chop four of the radishes and, with the yoghurt, stir them into the cheese mixture. Spoon the dip into a dish and garnish with the remaining cheese and the radish cut into a flower or sliced.

Cucumber Dip
Serves 4

8 fl oz (225 ml) natural yoghurt
4 in (10 cm) cucumber, finely diced
few sprigs of fresh mint, chopped

Combine all the ingredients and serve.

Curd Cheese and Herb Dip
Serves 4

5 fl oz (150 ml) natural yoghurt
4 oz (100 g) curd cheese
4 tablespoons freshly chopped herbs (parsley, mint, basil, tarragon, chives)
salt to taste

Beat together the ingredients, chill and serve.

Walnut, Mustard and Cheese Dip
Serves 4

8 oz (225 g) cheese (Wensleydale is ideal), grated
salt and freshly ground black pepper to taste
pinch cayenne pepper
2 teaspoons prepared English mustard
2 oz (50 g) chopped walnuts
5 fl oz (150 ml) natural yoghurt

Combine all the ingredients and beat them together. Chill and serve.

PÂTÉS

Demivegetarian pâtés are generally quicker and simpler to prepare than a standard meat pâté and lower in fat content. Here are four recipes: the first is for a mushroom and cheese vegetarian pâté, the second and third for very quick-to-prepare fish pâtés, and the fourth for a more complicated but delicious chicken and vegetable terrine which makes an ideal starter for a special dinner party.

Mushroom Pâté
Serves 4

8 oz (225 g) button mushrooms
4 oz (100 g) butter
2 teaspoons finely grated onion
1 oz (25 g) fresh brown breadcrumbs
4 oz (100 g) curd cheese or low-fat cream cheese
parsley sprigs
1 teaspoon lemon juice
salt and freshly ground black pepper to taste

Slice the mushrooms, reserving a few slices for garnish. Melt 2 oz (50 g) butter in a saucepan, add the mushrooms and onion and sauté gently until soft. Stir in the breadcrumbs and allow to cool. Soften the remaining butter. In a blender combine the cooked mixture, the softened butter, the curd or low-fat cream cheese, parsley, lemon juice and seasoning. Blend until almost smooth. Chill until required. Serve garnished with the mushroom slices.

Kipper Pâté
Serves 6

4 kipper fillets
1 clove garlic, crushed
2 tablespoons natural yoghurt
1 teaspoon lemon juice
freshly ground black pepper to taste

Poach the kipper fillets in water for 4–5 minutes. Drain, remove the skin and chill the fillets. Place the fish in a food processor with the garlic, and blend until smooth. Stir in the yoghurt and lemon juice to give a smooth consistency and season with black pepper.

Salmon or Tuna Pâté
Serves 4

7½ oz (213 g) tin pink salmon or tuna fish, drained, bones and skin removed
8 oz (225 g) plain cottage cheese
3 oz (75 g) cucumber, finely chopped (reserve some for garnish)
1 tablespoon lemon juice
freshly ground black pepper to taste

Mash the salmon or tuna fish, add the cottage cheese, cucumber and lemon juice. Mix thoroughly and season with pepper. Pile the mixture into a small dish, smooth the top and garnish with reserved cucumber.

Chicken and Vegetable Terrine with Green Peppercorns
Serves 6

2 lbs (1 kg) courgettes, grated or finely shredded
salt and freshly ground black pepper to taste
2 tablespoons olive oil
1 small onion, finely chopped
1 clove garlic, crushed
8 oz (225 g) chicken, finely chopped
4 eggs, beaten
½ pint (275 ml) double cream
2 tablespoons chopped fresh tarragon
2 teaspoons green peppercorns
young spinach leaves, blanched or leaves from the centre of a lettuce

Line a greased loaf tin with lightly greased greaseproof paper, making sure that it fits the corners well. Put the courgettes into a colander and sprinkle generously with salt. Leave them to drain for 30 minutes, then rinse them to remove the salt and pat them dry on a clean teatowel. Gently fry the onion and garlic in the butter for 3 minutes until they are just soft. Add the courgettes and cook gently for 6 minutes. Cool, then mix the cooked courgettes and onion with the chicken, eggs, cream, tarragon, green peppercorns, and salt and black pepper. Spoon the mixture into the prepared loaf tin and cover it with a piece of lightly greased foil. Stand the loaf tin in a roasting tin and add hot water to come halfway up the sides of the tin. Cook in the oven on 180°C (350°F, gas mark 4) for 1½ hours until just firm to the touch. Lift the loaf tin out of the water and allow it to cool. Carefully tip off any liquid from the top of the cooked terrine. When cold, unmould the terrine onto a serving platter and arrange the spinach or lettuce leaves decoratively over the top.

Note: This terrine has a better flavour if it is made in advance and chilled for at least 12 hours before eating.

Sicilian Cauliflower
Serves 4

This Mediterranean recipe has a wonderful flavour and makes a good starter or a light lunch dish.

1 medium-sized cauliflower
4 tablespoons olive oil
1 large onion, chopped
12 black olives, stoned and sliced
6 anchovy fillets, chopped
salt and freshly ground black pepper to taste
½ tablespoon chopped fresh rosemary (if available)
5 fl oz (150 ml) coarse red wine

Divide the cauliflower into even sized florets. Pour a little olive oil into a deepish heavy pan with a lid. Add some of the onion, olives and anchovies. Add a layer of cauliflower, a sprinkling of oil and very little salt and pepper. Repeat the layers. Finish by pouring the remaining oil and the red wine over the top. Cover and cook gently until the cauliflower is tender. The liquid should have more or less evaporated by the time the cauliflower is done, but be prepared to raise the heat to boil it away. Turn onto a hot serving dish and serve.

Hot Crab and Avocado
Serves 2 – 4

Crabmeat, avocado flesh, cream cheese and hot sauce are combined and the mixture used to fill the avocado skins. The stuffed avocados are briefly baked before serving.

2 small avocados
2 tablespoons lemon juice
8 oz (225 g) crabmeat (fresh, frozen or tinned)
5 oz (150 g) cream cheese
2 teaspoons tomato purée
few drops Tabasco or other hot pepper sauce
salt and freshly ground black pepper to taste

Preheat oven to 180°C (350°F, gas mark 5). Halve the avocados and remove the stones. Scoop out the centres and place the skins on one side. Mash the avocado flesh with the lemon juice. Add the remaining ingredients and mix well. Fill each avocado shell until it is nicely rounded. Bake for 10 minutes or until the crab mixture is warmed through.

Welsh-Cheese-and-Strawberry-Filled Melon
Serves 4

2 small melons (ogen or charentais)
4 oz (100 g) Caerphilly cheese, cut into small cubes
2 in (5 cm) cucumber, diced
4 oz (100 g) wild strawberries or cultivated strawberries, quartered

DRESSING
1 tablespoon vinegar
3 tablespoons olive oil
½ teaspoon mustard powder
salt and freshly ground black pepper to taste
1 teaspoon sugar

Cut the melons in half horizontally and scoop out the seeds. Set the halves aside. Mix together the cheese, cucumber and strawberries. Pile this mixture into the melon halves. Put all the dressing ingredients in a screw-top jar and shake well. Pour the dressing over the melon filling. Serve chilled.

Fresh Pineapple and Prawns
Serves 6

Any starter with the name 'cocktail' is normally not to my liking since it usually portends a meal such as prawn cocktail, steak and Black Forest gâteau. The recipe given here relies on fresh pineapple to lift it out of the steakhouse syndrome, so use tinned pineapple only as a second best.

1 small fresh pineapple, peeled and cut into small chunks
8 oz (225 g) black grapes, halved and seeded
1 lb (450 g) peeled prawns
4 tablespoons mayonnaise
2 tablespoons whipping cream, lightly whipped
salt and freshly ground black pepper to taste
1 small lettuce

Combine the first six ingredients and serve on a bed of torn lettuce leaves in individual bowls.

Moules Marinière
Serves 4

Moules Marinière is quick to prepare and very tasty. The quality of mussels available has improved significantly in the last few years and often the home-grown variety, particularly from along the Welsh coast and the Scottish islands, is as good as those imported from France and Holland. Supplies from the Wash are also improving. Moules Marinière makes a robust starter or a light meal in itself.

1 oz (25 g) butter
1 medium onion, finely chopped
1 clove garlic, crushed
½ pint (275 ml) dry white wine or stock
2 tablespoons lemon juice
3 bay leaves
salt and freshly ground black pepper to taste
4 pints (2.2 litres) live mussels, scrubbed and scraped
3 tablespoons freshly chopped parsley

Melt the butter in a large saucepan and lightly fry the onion and garlic. Add the wine or stock, lemon juice, bay leaves, salt and black pepper, and bring to the boil. Add the mussels all at once, cover and cook over a high heat, shaking the pan occasionally to ensure even cooking. When all the mussels have opened (you must discard any that have not) transfer them to a heated serving dish, reserving the liquid. Boil up the liquid, add the parsley and stir. Adjust the seasoning and pour the liquid over the mussels.

Sherry-Marinated Herring
Serves 6

Serve marinated herring as a starter or as a main dish with a salad. The herrings need 48–72 hours' marinating time, so you need to plan ahead if you wish to serve this dish.

4 herrings, filleted
½ oz (12.5 g) butter
1 clove garlic, crushed
1 small yellow pepper
1 small green pepper
14 oz (397 g) tin tomatoes, chopped
¼ pint (150 ml) wine vinegar
¼ pint (150 ml) medium sherry
1 tablespoon light brown sugar
salt and freshly ground black pepper to taste

Cut each herring into 2 in (5 cm) pieces and place them in a deep dish. Melt the butter and fry the garlic and peppers for a few minutes. Add the tomatoes and simmer until the peppers are tender. Add the liquids and sugar and stir until the sugar has dissolved. Season with salt and black pepper. Pour the marinade over the fish and mix well. Cover and refrigerate for at least 48–72 hours. Serve the fish and marinade together with fresh French bread.

Herring and Red Pepper Brochettes

Serves 4

Filleted herring is cut into pieces, skewered with quarters of red pepper, brushed with a marinade and grilled. Simple but delicious, and an appetizing starter.

4 herrings, filleted but not skinned
1 large red pepper, cut into 1 in (2.5 cm) squares
3 tablespoons sunflower oil
juice and grated rind of 1 orange
juice and grated rind of 1 lemon
1 tablespoon freshly chopped fresh thyme or parsley
salt and freshly ground black pepper to taste

Cut each herring crosswise into four pieces and thread them alternately with the pepper squares on four short skewers. Combine the remaining ingredients and liberally brush the fish and peppers with the mixture. Grill 16 brochettes under a moderate heat for about 10 minutes, turning the skewers and brushing the fish with the marinade every now and again.

Note: For a main dish, double the quantities and serve with rice and salad. This is also an ideal dish for a barbecue.

Chicken Wings in Garlic and Lemon Sauce
Serves 4

Chicken wings are cheap and sometimes only used for stock by the cook who portions a whole chicken. There is, however, quite a lot of flesh on them and this recipe gives them plenty of flavour.

8 chicken wings cut in half
2 cloves garlic, finely chopped
juice of 2 lemons
salt to taste

Put the wings in a small bowl and sprinkle them with the garlic, lemon juice and salt. Using your fingers, make sure each wing is coated in the marinade. Cover and set aside for 1 hour. Put the chicken and marinade into a heavy saucepan in which the pieces will fit in one layer. Add enough water barely to cover the chicken and bring to the boil. Cover the pan, reduce the heat and simmer for 15 minutes. Towards the end of the cooking time the cooking liquor should have reduced to a thickish sauce. If not, remove the pan lid for the last few minutes. Serve four chicken pieces per portion and pour some of the sauce from the pan over each helping.

Chicken Parcels Wrapped in Nori Seaweed
Serves 4

This is a slightly tricky recipe to put together, but once you have got the hang of it, it makes a very nice hors d'oeuvre. Nori is a purple seaweed sold in paper-thin sheets. It is used extensively in Japanese cooking for seasoning, garnishing and wrapping. It is available from grocery stores which stock Japanese products and is sold in packets of 10 sheets.

8 oz.(225 g) chicken breast, cooked and boned
2 tablespoons saké or dry white wine
2 tablespoons soya sauce
1 sheet nori seaweed cut crosswise into ½ in (1.25 cm) wide strips
1 egg white
2 tablespoons vegetable oil

Cut the chicken meat into 2 × 1 × ¼ in (5 × 2.5 × 0.5 cm) pieces. Combine the saké and soya sauce and use them to marinate the chicken pieces for 1 hour. One at a time roll up each chicken piece like a carpet. Secure the roll with a strip of nori seaweed dipped in egg white and fixed with a cocktail stick. Repeat for each piece of chicken. Heat half the oil in a frying pan or wok and lightly fry half the chicken parcels. Repeat with the remaining oil and chicken parcels.

Paper-Wrapped Prawns
Serves 4 as a side dish

This Chinese recipe is traditionally made with large fresh uncooked prawns. Served piping hot, they make an exciting side dish or starter.

8 – 12 large prawns, shelled and any dark veins removed
1 teaspoon medium to sweet sherry
salt and freshly ground black pepper to taste
1 teaspoon peanut or vegetable oil
8 very thin slices fresh root ginger
2 spring onions, each cut into four pieces
8 mangetout
oil for deep frying

Put the prawns (halved lengthways if they are very large) in a small bowl. Add the sherry, salt and black pepper and mix well. Cut eight pieces of greaseproof paper 6 in (15 cm) square. Rub a light film of oil over both sides of the paper with your finger. Now make up the parcels, following the diagrams shown here. Heat the oil until it barely smokes. Deep-fry the paper parcels, folded side down, until the paper is lightly browned – about 1 minute. Drain the parcels on absorbent paper. Serve two parcels to a plate. To eat, unwrap the paper and remove the contents with chopsticks.

Note: The largest raw prawns are usually sold headless; peel them by pulling the legs up and over the back. Remove the black vein which runs down the length of the back to the tail.

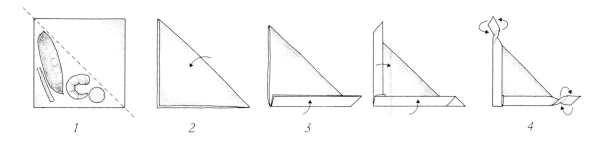

1   2   3   4

1 *Lay the squares flat and put a ration of prawns in the bottom lefthand corner of each, with a slice of ginger, a piece of spring onion and a mangetout.*
2 *Make up the parcels by folding each square in half diagonally, to form a triangle.*
3 *Fold each open side in, crease the edge firmly and repeat.*
4 *Twist the corners like a toffee paper to make complete oilproof seal.*

Spinach, Mushroom and Crouton Salad

Serves 4

A first-course salad of dark green spinach leaves and white crunchy mushrooms and croutons.

8 oz (225 g) spinach
8 oz (225 g) small mushrooms
24 croutons (see below)
salt and black pepper to taste
juice of ½ lemon
6 tablespoons olive oil
2 tablespoons white wine vinegar

Wash the spinach and drain it well. Tear the leaves into large pieces, discarding the stalks. Pile the spinach in a bowl. Wipe and slice the mushrooms, and then squeeze the lemon juice over them. Put the salt and pepper in a small bowl, add the olive oil and wine vinegar and whisk until blended. Scatter the mushrooms and croutons over the spinach, pour the dressing over the lot, toss thoroughly and serve.

CROUTONS

To make croutons you need good, firm bread. A single ⅜ in (1 cm) slice from a 2 lb (1 kg) loaf will make enough croutons for three to four people.

Take a 5 in (12 cm) pan, add vegetable oil to a depth of ⅜ in (1 cm) and place over a medium heat. Meanwhile remove the crusts from the bread and cut the slices into ⅜ in (1 cm) cubes. When the oil has just begun to haze, test its temperature by dropping in one of the bread cubes. It should turn quite rapidly to a golden-brown colour. Rescue the cube from the oil, reduce the heat slightly and drop in enough of the bread cubes to cover loosely the bottom of the pan. When these cubes are nicely browned, lift them out with a slotted spoon and drain them on absorbent kitchen paper. Repeat the process until all the bread cubes are used. Croutons are best eaten fresh but will keep for a day or two in an airtight container.

SALADS

Raw vegetables and fruit contain all their original nutrients and fibre since none is lost in cooking; they also contain enzymes which assist digestion. Apart from being nutritious, salads are quick to prepare, economical if you use vegetables and fruits in season, colourful and delicious to eat. Salads thus play an important role in a demivegetarian diet and at least one meal a day should be accompanied by a side salad or, in warmer months, should include a salad as a main dish.

The basic ingredients of nearly all the salads given here are vegetables and/or fruit but, in keeping with the demivegetarian idea, some contain cheese, fish or chicken. Each recipe is suitable for inclusion in a high-fibre, low-fat diet. If a salad requires a dressing, with the exception of French dressing (see p.18), the ingredients and the method of preparation are included in the individual recipes. For those on a very low-fat diet the amount of oil used in a dressing may be reduced. Remember, however, to reduce accordingly any accompanying lemon juice or vinegar.

Remember also that it is best to use vegetables and fruit in season. In this way you will buy them at their cheapest and tastiest. This is not the case just for locally grown produce but for imported vegetables and fruit as well. The same kind of imported produce will ripen at different times of the year depending on the country of origin, so it is worth finding a good greengrocer who is aware of changing market patterns and who knows when to buy produce from overseas suppliers.

White Cabbage and Fruit Coleslaw
Serves 4

This is a crunchy winter salad that makes a good low-fat alternative to the more familiar Waldorf salad.

½ medium-sized white cabbage, finely shredded
French dressing to taste (see p. 18)
4 celery sticks, cut into thin matchstick-length strips
2 eating apples, cored and chopped
4 oz (100 g) grapes, halved and seeded
2 oz (50 g) chopped walnuts
1 tablespoon chopped chives (optional)
salt and freshly ground black pepper to taste

Put the shredded cabbage into a salad bowl and stir in sufficient dressing just to moisten it. Add the other ingredients and mix well.

Chicory and Orange Salad

Serves 4

The flavour of chicory goes well with orange or grapefruit. Choose chicory heads that are tight and with unblemished pointed leaves. Yoghurt is used in this recipe as a low-fat alternative to mayonnaise or French dressing.

2 heads chicory, finely chopped
1 small onion (red if possible), thinly sliced
1 medium orange, peeled and segmented
2 oz (50 g) chopped walnuts
6 oz (180 g) natural yoghurt
salt and freshly ground black pepper to taste

Combine the chicory, onion, orange and walnuts. Stir in the yoghurt, season with salt and grind black pepper over the top.

Celeriac, Beansprout and Mangetout Salad

Serves 4–6

Celeriac is neglected in this country but it has a fine flavour and makes a good salad ingredient. The French often use it to advantage in *crudités*. Celeriac looks like a small swede with a wrinkled skin. In this winter salad it is combined with beansprouts and mangetout peas. Buy only very young mangetout with flat pods.

1 medium-size head celeriac
juice of 1 lemon
4 oz (100 g) small mangetout, washed and drained
4 oz (100 g) fresh beansprouts, washed and drained
5 tablespoons olive oil
juice of ½ lemon
pinch caster sugar
salt and freshly ground black pepper to taste
1 clove garlic, crushed
2 tablespoons chopped parsley

Peel the celeriac and grate or shred it coarsely; mix it with the lemon juice immediately to prevent it from discolouring. Combine the celeriac, mangetout and beansprouts in a salad bowl. For the dressing, mix the olive oil, lemon juice, sugar, salt and black pepper, garlic and parsley. Spoon the dressing over the vegetables and toss together.

Avocado and Pink Grapefruit Salad

Serves 4

This recipe and introduction is supplied by Paddy Byrne, my partner in the Everyman Bistro. The salad is one of simple contrast, soft green set against soft pink. The almost excessive richness of the avocado is cut here by the sharpness of the grapefruit, which in its turn is made to taste sweet by having dribbled over it at the last moment a small quantity of even sharper vinegar.

4 medium Hass avocados, peeled and sliced
salt and freshly ground black pepper to taste
2 pink grapefruit, peeled, with all traces of pith removed
4 tablespoons olive oil
3 teaspoons wine or cider vinegar

Arrange the slices of avocado radial fashion on four small plain plates. Season well with the salt and black pepper. Separate the grapefruit into segments and cut each segment in half. Pile the grapefruit pieces in the centre of each plate. Dress the avocado with the oil and just before serving sprinkle the grapefruit with the vinegar.

Chilled Aubergine Salad

Serves 4

Cooked cold aubergines make a good and unusual salad ingredient. Try them in a rice or bean salad or as a main ingredient, as in this recipe.

2 medium-size aubergines, cut into ¾ in (2 cm) cubes
salt
6 oz (175 g) French shallots, finely chopped
6 tablespoons olive oil
1 clove garlic, crushed
finely grated rind of ½ orange
6 tablespoons dry French white wine
freshly ground black pepper

GARNISH
peeled chopped orange segments
sprigs of fresh dill

Put the cubed aubergines into a colander and sprinkle generously with salt. Leave on one side to drain for half an hour, then pat the cubes dry on absorbent paper. Fry the shallots gently in 2 tablespoons of the olive oil for 3 minutes. Add the garlic and fry gently for a further minute. Add the remaining oil and then add the aubergines to the pan; fry gently for 3–4 minutes. Add the orange rind,

Monkfish and Pear Salad (page 56)

Asparagus with Tarragon and Walnut Sauce (page 62)

white wine, salt and black pepper. Simmer gently until the aubergine is just tender. Allow to cool and then chill. Spoon the mixture onto four small serving plates and garnish with orange segments and feathery pieces of dill.

Brussels Sprout and Apple Salad
Serves 4

For some reason many people do not like Brussels sprouts, perhaps because as children they were forced to eat overcooked, soggy specimens, but sprouts are delicious both raw and cooked. Buy ones that are a good green colour and not too large. Cook them in a pan with only a small amount of water (about 1 in or 2.5 cm deep) for 7–8 minutes, depending on their size. As soon as they are just tender, drain them and serve. Brussels sprouts are also surprisingly good in salads. Try them in this recipe or the one below.

2 tablespoons red wine vinegar
4 tablespoons olive oil
2 cloves garlic, crushed
1 teaspoon prepared mustard
1 tablespoon finely chopped fresh sage or parsley
salt and freshly ground black pepper to taste
1 eating apple, cored and sliced
juice of 1 lemon
4 spring onions, trimmed and chopped
¾ lb (350 g) Brussels sprouts, trimmed and finely shredded

Combine the vinegar, oil, garlic, mustard, sage or parsley, and salt and black pepper. Mix well together. Toss the apple slices in the lemon juice. In a serving bowl combine the spring onions, sprouts, apple slices and dressing. Toss well and serve.

Brussels Sprout and Carrot Salad
Serves 4

1 lb (450 g) Brussels sprouts
1 tablespoon finely chopped onion
2 medium carrots, grated
2 tablespoons sultanas
French dressing to taste (see p. 18)

Wash the sprouts and remove a slice from the base of each one. Shred coarsely. Mix with the finely chopped onion, grated raw carrot and sultanas. Stir in sufficient French dressing to moisten.

Simple Cucumber Salad
Serves 4

A refreshing and soothing salad that is good with spicy hot dishes.

*1 medium-sized cucumber
1 teaspoon salt
salt and freshly ground black pepper to taste
1 tablespoon caster sugar
1 tablespoon wine vinegar
3 tablespoons vegetable or olive oil
4 tablespoons natural yoghurt
2 tablespoons chopped chives or parsley*

Slice the cucumber. Place the slices in a colander and sprinkle them with a teaspoon of salt. Leave them for an hour to allow any excess water to be drawn out. Rinse the slices in cold water and dry well. Arrange them in a serving dish. Put salt and black pepper in a bowl, add the sugar and vinegar and mix well to dissolve the seasonings. Whisk in the oil, then the yoghurt and most of the chives or parsley. Pour or spoon the dressing over the cucumber. Sprinkle the remaining chopped chives or parsley over the top.

Cherry and Walnut Salad
Serves 4

This unusual savoury fruit salad may be served as a starter or a side dish.

*12 oz (350 g) black cherries
1 medium orange
½ Cos lettuce, separated into leaves
French dressing to taste (see p. 18)
2 oz (50 g) chopped walnuts*

Wash, halve and stone the cherries, reserving a few whole ones with stalks for garnish. Peel the orange, removing all the pith, and slice thinly with a sharp knife. Arrange the lettuce leaves round the outside of a shallow serving dish and place the orange slices on top. Toss the cherries in a little French dressing, add the walnuts and pile the mixture in the centre of the dish. Garnish with the whole cherries.

Cucumber with Sesame
Ginger Dressing
Serves 4

This recipe is provided by Paddy Byrne, my partner in the Everyman Bistro. The sesame ginger dressing goes well with any vegetable *crudités* but it is especially good with cucumber.

2 tablespoons tahini
2 tablespoons natural yoghurt or water
1 tablespoon sesame oil
1 teaspoon vinegar
1 teaspoon shoyu or soya sauce
1 clove garlic, crushed
1 almond-sized piece of fresh ginger, peeled and crushed
dash of hot pepper sauce
freshly ground black pepper to taste
1/2 large cucumber
1 teaspoon sesame seeds to garnish

Combine all the ingredients except the cucumber and sesame seeds in a small bowl. Mix them well together and pile the mixture in the centre of a large serving plate. Cut the cucumber down the middle and remove the seeds with the back of a spoon. Cut the cucumber into strips 3 in (8 cm) long and arrange these around the mound of dressing like the spokes of a wheel. Sprinkle sesame seeds over the top.

VARIATION

Instead of the cucumber, use 12 oz (350 g) beansprouts. Stir the shoots well into the dressing and then sprinkle the mixture with the sesame seeds.

Chinese Brown Rice Salad
Serves 4

A substantial and nutritious salad with a well-flavoured dressing.

8 oz (225 g) cooked brown rice
10 1/2 oz (300 g) tin bamboo shoots, drained and sliced
2 oz (50 g) button mushrooms, wiped and sliced
4 oz (100 g) beansprouts, rinsed and drained
1 bunch spring onions, trimmed and chopped
2 oz (50 g) cooked beans (red beans, chickpeas, broad beans, etc., or sweetcorn)
4 tablespoons medium sherry
1 1/2 tablespoons natural soya sauce
2 tablespoons wine vinegar
3 tablespoons vegetable oil (sesame seed oil is ideal)

Combine the rice, bamboo shoots, mushrooms, beansprouts, spring onions, and beans or sweetcorn in a salad bowl. Mix together the sherry, soya sauce, vinegar and oil and pour this dressing over the rice salad. Toss well and serve.

Beetroot, Apple and Yoghurt Salad
Serves 4

I particularly like beetroot, so this salad is one of my favourites. It is especially good in early to midsummer when beetroots are small and sweet.

1 lb (450 g) cooked beetroot, diced
1 eating apple, cored and grated
1 small onion (preferably red), finely sliced
juice of ½ lemon
2 teaspoons horseradish sauce
¼ pint (150 ml) natural yoghurt
1 tablespoon chopped chives or spring onions to garnish

Combine the beetroot, apple, onion and lemon juice. Stir the horseradish sauce into the yoghurt and then pour it over the salad. Mix well and chill before serving. Serve garnished with the chopped chives or spring onions.

Smoked Mackerel Salad
Serves 4–6

A delicious, nutritious and colourful mix of smoked fish, cheese, apple, cucumber and beetroot. Serve as a main dish or as a light meal with bread and a green salad.

1 lb (450 g) smoked mackerel fillets, skinned and diced
1 red apple, cored and diced
2 in (5 cm) cucumber, diced
1 oz (25 g) Cheddar cheese, diced
2 oz (50 g) cooked beetroot, diced
1 tablespoon olive oil
2 tablespoons wine or cider vinegar
pinch mustard powder
pinch brown sugar
salt and freshly ground black pepper to taste
finely chopped parsley to garnish

Combine the smoked mackerel, apple, cucumber, cheese and beetroot in a salad bowl. Mix together the remaining ingredients and pour them over the salad just before serving. Toss well and garnish with parsley.

Greek Salad
Serves 4–6

For many people this salad, with its taste of olive oil and its mix of olives, tomatoes and feta cheese, will bring back memories of long lunches on sunny Greek islands.

1 lettuce
2 large tomatoes, sliced
4 oz (100 g) black olives
2 oz (50 g) tin anchovies, coarsely chopped
4 oz (100 g) feta cheese, cubed
4 tablespoons olive oil
2 tablespoons wine vinegar
½ teaspoon crushed dried oregano or 2 teaspoons chopped fresh oregano
salt and freshly ground black pepper to taste

Separate the outer leaves of the lettuce, wash and drain them and arrange them around the outer edge of a salad bowl. Wash, drain and coarsely shred the inner leaves and place them in the middle of the bowl. On top arrange the tomatoes, olives, anchovies and feta cheese. Mix together the olive oil, vinegar, oregano, salt and black pepper. Pour this dressing over the salad and serve.

New Potato Salad with Blue Cheese Dressing
Serves 4

Much of the flavour and vitamin C in new potatoes (such as Jersey Royals) lies just below the skin, so the potatoes are best cooked with their skins on. Wash them in cold running water and then cook them in boiling water. Small varieties will take only 6–7 minutes to cook. Drain well and, if you wish, rub off the skins, although there is no real need to do this.

1 lb (450 g) new potatoes
1 tablespoon lemon juice
2 tablespoons mayonnaise
4 oz (100 g) soft blue cheese
2 tablespoons thick natural yoghurt
2 tablespoons milk
salt and freshly ground black pepper to taste
1 oz (25 g) toasted pine kernels
½ small cucumber, cut into ½ in (1 cm) cubes

Cook the potatoes with the lemon juice in sufficient boiling water to cover them. Drain and while still warm gently mix in the mayonnaise. Set aside to cool. In a food blender or processor blend together the cheese, yoghurt, milk, salt and black pepper. In a serving bowl combine the pine kernels and cucumber with the potatoes, reserving a few pine kernels for garnishing. Pour the dressing over the potatoes and garnish with the reserved pine kernels.

Chinese Salad with Hot Dressing
Serves 4

Shredded and sliced raw vegetables are covered with a stir-fried dressing of olive oil, chicken strips, water chestnuts, ginger and soya sauce.

½ large lettuce, shredded
2 large carrots, peeled and cut into matchsticks
½ medium cucumber, peeled, seeded and thinly sliced
6 spring onions, chopped
6 tablespoons olive oil
1 clove garlic, crushed
8 oz (225 g) cooked chicken, cut into thin strips
3 water chestnuts, thinly sliced
1 tablespoon soya sauce
salt and freshly ground black pepper to taste
2 pieces preserved stem ginger, finely chopped

Combine the lettuce, carrots and cucumber in a salad bowl. Fry the spring onions gently in the olive oil for 2–3 minutes. Add the garlic, chicken and water chestnuts, turn up the heat and stir-fry for 1–2 minutes. Remove the pan from the heat and add the soya sauce, salt, black pepper and ginger. Pour this mixture over the salad and serve immediately.

Skate and Fresh Spinach Salad
Serves 4

A most unusual but refreshing and tasty combination of ingredients.

8 oz (225 g) skate wings
¼ pint (150 ml) water
1 tablespoon lemon juice
1 tablespoon butter or polyunsaturated margarine
1 tablespoon sunflower oil
4 slices wholemeal bread, cut into cubes
6 oz (175 g) small spinach leaves, trimmed and washed
1 avocado, skinned and sliced
2 tablespoons French dressing (see p.18)

Place the skate in a shallow pan, cover it with water, add the lemon juice and poach for 5–6 minutes. Drain, flake the flesh from the bones and chill. Melt the butter or margarine and the oil and quickly sauté the bread until crisp and golden. In a large bowl mix together the fish, spinach and avocado. Pour the dressing over the mixture and toss carefully. Top with the croutons and serve immediately.

English Cheese and Rice Salad
Serves 4 – 6

Apart from having to cook the rice this salad is simple and quick to prepare. It is normally enjoyed by children who like the cheese and the sweetness of the dates and pineapple. Served on its own with a green salad, it makes a convenient light meal. For variation try other types of cheese; also try adding roasted nuts to the salad.

6 oz (175 g) long-grain brown or white rice
4 tablespoons French dressing (see p.18)
2 oz (50 g) Sage Derby cheese, diced
2 oz (50 g) Leicester cheese, diced
1 stick celery, chopped
2 spring onions, chopped
4 fresh dates, sliced
8 oz (225 g) tin pineapple slices, drained and chopped, or fresh pineapple, cubed
salt and freshly ground black pepper to taste

Cook the rice until it is just tender. Drain, rinse well in cold water and then toss it in the French dressing. Leave to cool. When cold, mix in the remaining ingredients.

Cracked Wheat and Smoked Haddock Salad
Serves 4 – 6

This combination of fish, wheat and vegetables is protein- and vitamin-rich. Serve it as a robust winter salad. Cracked wheat is simply wheat grains that have been crushed and par boiled. For quicker cooking bulgar wheat or couscous may be substituted.

6 oz (175 g) cracked wheat
1 lb (450 g) smoked haddock fillet, skinned and cubed
3 sticks celery, chopped
3 spring onions, chopped
2 tomatoes, sliced
6 tablespoons French dressing (see p.18)
1 tablespoon finely chopped mint
salt and freshly ground black pepper to taste
fresh mint to garnish

Place the cracked wheat in a large bowl, cover with water and leave to soak for 2 – 3 hours or overnight. Place the haddock in a pan, cover with water and poach for 4 – 5 minutes. Drain and chill. Check the wheat is tender, then drain it and fold in the cooked fish, celery, onions and tomatoes. Stir in the dressing, adjust the seasonings if necessary and garnish with mint leaves.

Monkfish and Pear Salad
Serves 4 – 6

Monkfish is popular nowadays but alas no longer cheap, so this salad is only for special occasions, although the substitution of cod or haddock could allow you to use it more often. Serve it as a starter to a dinner or as the main course of a light cold meal. The other main ingredient in this recipe is pears. They are often overlooked as a salad ingredient but they go well in cheese and fish combinations.

1 1/2 lb (675 g) monkfish fillets, skinned and cubed
1/2 pint (275 ml) water
2 tablespoons lemon juice
salt and freshly ground black pepper to taste
2 dessert pears, cored and sliced
2 oz (50 g) walnut pieces
1 bunch watercress, roughly chopped
1 clove garlic, crushed (optional)
2 tablespoons tarragon vinegar or other vinegar
3 tablespoons sunflower oil
lemon wedges (optional)

Gently poach the fish in the water with the lemon juice, salt and black pepper for 4 – 5 minutes. Drain and chill the fish. Mix together the pears, walnut pieces and watercress and add them to the chilled fish. To make the dressing, put the garlic, vinegar and oil in a screw-top jar and shake well. Pour the dressing over the salad. Toss, season to taste and serve accompanied with lemon wedges if desired.

VEGETABLE
DISHES

Vegetables served as the principal ingredient of a main dish or as an accompaniment to a chicken, fish or dairy dish, or uncooked in salads make an important contribution to the demivegetarian diet. In this chapter we deal with cooked vegetables; for raw vegetable recipes see pp. 46–54.

The recipes given here are, with a few exceptions, vegetable-only dishes. Those that are not contain small quantities of chicken or fish. The recipes are divided into mixed or single vegetable dishes. The latter normally contain explanatory notes on buying and preparing the vegetable in question.

There are three main rules to follow when cooking vegetables. First, buy good-quality specimens in season; second, wash them thoroughly and, third, cook them in the minimum of time and liquid required to make them tender so they retain their colour and texture.

Also given in this chapter are two savoury recipes that use fruit as one of their ingredients. They are included to demonstrate the demivegetarian view that a mixed diet, containing widely varied foods, each eaten in moderation is usually a good one.

STIR-FRIED VEGETABLES

Stir-frying is an excellent method of cooking vegetables. They are cooked so quickly in their own juices that very little of the nutritional content is lost. The important thing to remember is to have all the ingredients chopped and ready before you start cooking. When the stir-fry is ready it should be served immediately. Five stir-fry recipes are given here. The first two make good side dishes, although with the addition of shredded cooked chicken and/or peeled prawns they can be served as a main course; the other three will individually serve four people as a vegetarian main or side dish with rice.

Simple Stir-Fry
Serves 4

4 tablespoons vegetable oil
1 teaspoon peeled and grated fresh ginger root
6 oz (175 g) Chinese leaves, shredded
6 oz (175 g) Brussels sprouts, finely chopped
6 oz (175 g) leeks, finely chopped
6 oz (175 g) cauliflower florets
natural soya sauce to taste
freshly ground black pepper to taste (optional)

Heat the oil in a wok or deep frying pan and sauté the ginger for less than a minute. Add the prepared vegetables and stir-fry for 4–5 minutes. The vegetables should remain slightly crunchy. Add the soya sauce while continuing to stir the vegetables. Add black pepper if you wish. Serve immediately.

Chilli-Hot Stir-Fry
Serves 4

4 tablespoons vegetable oil
6 oz (175 g) carrots, cut into julienne strips
6 oz (175 g) celery, finely chopped
6 oz (175 g) green peppers, seeded, cored and cut into julienne strips
6 oz (175 g) bean sprouts
salt and freshly ground black pepper to taste
1 teaspoon chilli sauce

Heat the oil in a wok or deep frying pan. Add the carrots, celery and green peppers and stir-fry for 3–4 minutes. Add the bean sprouts and cook for a further minute. Season with salt and black pepper and stir in the chilli sauce. Serve immediately.

Vegetable and Lettuce Stir-Fry
Serves 4

1 medium onion, peeled and thinly sliced
1 medium red pepper, seeded and cut into thin strips
1 medium yellow pepper, seeded and cut into thin strips
1 large clove garlic, peeled and finely chopped
1 medium-sized leek, split, cleaned and cut into thin strips
4 tablespoons olive oil
1 tablespoon sesame seeds
4 oz (100 g) bean sprouts
6 oz (175 g) iceberg lettuce, finely shredded
salt and freshly ground black pepper to taste
2 teaspoons cornflour
4 tablespoons chicken stock or water
4 tablespoons dry sherry
2 teaspoons natural soya sauce
chopped fresh coriander to garnish

In a wok or large, deep frying pan stir-fry the onion, garlic and leek in half the olive oil for 4 minutes over a brisk heat. Add the sesame seeds, bean sprouts, shredded lettuce and salt and black pepper. Stir-fry for 2 minutes. Blend the cornflour with the stock or water, sherry and soya sauce; add the mixture to the pan and stir over the heat for 1–2 minutes until the sauce has thickened slightly and is glossy. Serve piping hot and sprinkled with chopped coriander.

Stir-Fry Broccoli and Tofu
Serves 4

Tofu or beancurd (the names are interchangeable) is very useful in stir-fry dishes. It absorbs the flavours of other ingredients and adds substance to vegetable meals. Pressed tofu is easier to stir-fry than the more fragile fresh tofu, but the best of all for stir-frying is, tofu that has already been deep-fried. This can be bought in Chinese grocery shops. It is sold in about 4 in (10 cm) square, 1 in (2.5 cm) thick slabs and can be recognized by its slightly tough yellow outer skin.

2 large stalks broccoli
3 tablespoons vegetable oil
2 medium onions, coarsely chopped
3 cloves garlic, crushed
1 teaspoon grated fresh ginger
12 oz (350 g) tofu, drained and pressed
(or use deep-fried tofu)
1/4 teaspoon hot pepper sauce
2 tablespoons natural soya sauce

Separate the broccoli florets from the stalk and chop them. Peel the stalk and cut it diagonally into 1 in (2.5 cm) lengths. Heat the oil in a wok or large frying pan and stir-fry the onions, garlic, ginger and broccoli stalks until the onions are just softened. Add the broccoli florets and stir-fry for 2 minutes. Add the tofu and hot pepper sauce, stir well and then cover the wok or pan and cook over a low heat for 2–4 minutes. The broccoli stalks should be just firm to the bite. At the last minute stir in the soya sauce and serve immediately.

Stir-Fried Watercress and Chinese Mushrooms

Serves 4 as a side dish

Watercress is most often used in Britain as a salad ingredient but the Chinese use it as a vegetable. Its good flavour and rapid cooking time make watercress an ideal stir-fry ingredient.

2 bunches fresh green watercress
6 Chinese dried black mushrooms
2 tablespoons vegetable oil
2 oz (50 g) bamboo shoots, shredded
salt to taste
1 teaspoon sugar
1 in (2.5 cm) root ginger, peeled and chopped
1 tablespoon brandy (optional)

Trim off and discard the tougher stems of the watercress. Rinse and shake the leaves well. Put the mushrooms in a mixing bowl, cover them with boiling water and allow them to stand for 30 minutes. Drain, then squeeze them to remove excess moisture. Cut off and discard the tough stalks and finely chop the caps. Heat the oil in a frying pan or wok and add the bamboo shoots and mushrooms. Cook, stirring, over a high heat for about 1 minute. Add the watercress and stir. Add the salt, sugar and ginger and cook for 1 minute, stirring all the while. Add the brandy if used and cook for a further 5 seconds. Spoon the vegetables onto a serving dish, leaving any liquid in the pan. Reduce this over a high heat, then add the liquid that will have accumulated in the serving dish (rather a lot). Reduce it briefly and pour it over the vegetables.

Asparagus with Tarragon and Walnut Sauce

Serves 4

Asparagus should be eaten as soon as possible for its delicious flavour to be enjoyed. If kept too long after purchase, the spears become dry and woody. Choose spears that are the same length and thickness.

Asparagus needs careful cooking if it is to have a good colour and texture. Start by peeling the stems thinly with a potato peeler, then tie the spears in a bundle with a piece of string and stand them in a saucepan with sufficient boiling water to come about 2 in (5 cm) up the base of the stems. Invert a second saucepan of the same size over the top so that it fits neatly on the lower pan. Simmer until the asparagus is tender. The simmering time will depend on the thickness of the stems – stubbier spears will take 15 minutes upwards. The steam from the water in the saucepan will gently cook the tips without overcooking them. Do not throw the asparagus water away – it is full of goodness and can be used to give extra flavour to asparagus soup or stock.

Asparagus tips are delicious eaten raw in salads and the stalks can be used for soup. Nutritionally, asparagus is rich in vitamins A, B 1, B 2 and C.

For a delicious summertime meal try this recipe for asparagus with tarragon and walnut sauce.

1 1/2 lb (700 g) asparagus
1/2 oz (12.5 g) vegetable margarine or butter
1/2 oz (12.5 g) flour
1/4 pint (150 ml) fresh or skimmed milk
salt and freshly ground black pepper to taste
1 tablespoon finely chopped tarragon
1/2 oz (12.5 g) chopped walnuts
3 tablespoons asparagus cooking water

Prepare and cook the asparagus as described above. Melt the margarine or butter in a saucepan, stir in the flour and cook for less than a minute. Slowly add the milk, stirring all the time, and then season with salt and black pepper. Bring the mixture to the boil, reduce the heat and simmer for a few minutes until the sauce is thickened. Stir in the tarragon, walnuts and asparagus water. Simmer for a further 2 minutes. Drain the asparagus well and serve hot with the sauce.

Asparagus Nut Cases
Serves 6

5 oz (150 g) fresh brown breadcrumbs
4 oz (100 g) ground almonds
3 oz (75 g) butter or vegetable margarine
1 oz (25 g) flaked almonds, finely chopped
1 clove garlic, crushed
1/2 teaspoon dried mixed herbs
1 egg, beaten
1 oz (25 g) flour
1/4 pint (150 ml) fresh or skimmed milk
10 oz (300 g) tinned cut asparagus spears
(reserve the juice) or fresh asparagus
salt and freshly ground black pepper to taste

Preheat oven to 230°C (450°F, gas mark 8). If using fresh asparagus, prepare it as described on p. 00, then trim the spears into 1 in (2.5 cm) lengths. Butter well six 4 in (10 cm) patty tins.

To prepare the cases, mix together the breadcrumbs and ground almonds, and rub in 2 oz (50 g) butter or margarine. Stir in the almonds, garlic, herbs and egg to bind. Line the patty tins with the mixture. Bake for 15 minutes. Keep warm.

Meanwhile prepare the filling. Put 1 oz (25 g) butter or margarine, flour, milk and 1/4 pint (150 ml) asparagus juice or cooking water from the asparagus into a saucepan. Heat, stirring continuously, until the mixture boils and thickens. Drain any remaining juice from the asparagus into a saucepan. Heat, stirring continuously, until the mixture boils and thickens. Drain any remaining juice from the asparagus. Reserving a few pieces of asparagus, stir the remainder into the sauce and season with salt and black pepper. Reheat without boiling. Spoon the sauce into the pastry cases and garnish them with the reserved asparagus. Serve immediately.

Note: This recipe can alternatively be made in a single 8 in (20 cm) flan dish or ring.

Green Bean Gratin

Serves 4

Like most green beans, runner beans — or stick beans as they are otherwise known — should be eaten as young and as fresh as possible. When buying beans choose smaller pods, as the longer, fatter ones, especially those over 10 in (22.5 cm) in length, will be coarse and stringy. A good test of how fresh runner beans are is to snap the end off one — it should snap easily with a distinct crunch. Store the beans in the crisper drawer at the bottom of the refrigerator for a day or two, leaving them loose so they can breathe. Alternatively stand the stem ends in a little water and store them in a cool place but for no longer than 24 hours. The traditional way of preparing runner beans by slicing them is not always necessary. The small tender ones often look and taste better left whole or cut in half, their shape and size contrasting with the other vegetables in the dish. Whether served whole or sliced, they need topping and tailing first to remove the string from the side of the bean. Snap off the ends and pull off the string or use a small sharp knife or potato peeler to shave the sides. Runner beans are best steamed or cooked in a little boiling water for 5–8 minutes avoiding overcooking, as they become floppy and lose their crunchy texture if cooked too long. Overcooking also encourages the loss of vitamins in the cooking water. Runner beans are good vegetables to add to casseroles, stews or gratins; they can also be served in a vinaigrette dressing.

Green bean gratin is a delicious vegetable dish.

1 lb (450 g) young runner beans, topped, tailed and stringed
1 medium red or green pepper, seeded and cut into strips
3 small courgettes, thinly sliced
2 tablespoons olive or other vegetable oil
salt and freshly ground black pepper to taste
6 tablespoons fromage frais
2 oz (50 g) Cheddar cheese, grated

Cut the beans in half crosswise and cook them in boiling water for 5 minutes. Drain and rinse them in running water until cold. Preheat the oven to 180°C (350°F, gas mark 4). Sauté the pepper and courgettes in the oil until just softened. Transfer them to an ovenproof dish and add the beans. Season the vegetables with salt and black pepper and spread the *fromage frais* over them. Sprinkle the cheese over the top and bake the dish in the preheated oven for 15–20 minutes or until the top is golden brown.

Note: For a stronger-tasting dish distribute a few anchovies among the vegetables before topping with *fromage frais*.

Cauliflower Curry
Serves 4

Like most vegetables, cauliflowers should be bought as fresh as possible. Choose ones that have healthy green outer leaves and creamy-to-white compact heads without loose brown, grey or damaged florets. Many people overcook cauliflowers, especially when cooking them whole. The danger is to wait for the thick stalk to cook, which overcooks the florets. To avoid this, remove a plug from the stalk of the cauliflower, using a small, sharp, pointed knife. Stand the cauliflower in a saucepan containing about 2 in (5 cm) water, bring the water to the boil and cover the saucepan. The steam will gently cook the florets. This will take between 10 and 15 minutes, depending on the size of the cauliflower. A little lemon juice or a slice of lemon added to the cooking water helps to preserve the natural whiteness of the florets.

Cauliflower is delicious cut into florets, dipped in batter and then deep-fried, or eaten raw in salads or as part of a selection of *crudités*. Cauliflower is also delicious in curries, especially if the florets are not overcooked; they provide extra texture and flavour which contrast well with the other vegetables, as in the following recipe. Serve cauliflower curry with white or brown rice.

3 tablespoons olive or other vegetable oil
1 medium onion, finely chopped
1 medium aubergine, cut into 1/2 in (1 cm) cubes,
salted, pressed and rinsed
2–3 tablespoons mild curry powder or paste
12 oz (350 g) tomatoes, quartered
2 tablespoons plain flour
1 pint (550 ml) vegetable or chicken stock
salt and freshly ground black pepper to taste
1 small cauliflower, cut into florets
2 oz (50 g) seedless raisins
1 tablespoon chopped fresh coriander

Add the oil to a saucepan and sauté the onion, aubergine and curry powder for 2–3 minutes, stirring all the time. Add the tomatoes and sauté a further minute. Stir in the flour, stock, salt and black pepper. Cover and simmer for 8–10 minutes or until the aubergine is nearly tender. Add the cauliflower and raisins and cook a further 5–8 minutes or until the cauliflower is just tender but still crunchy. Serve garnished with chopped coriander.

Spaghetti Cauliflower Carbonade

Serves 4

A quick, flavoursome and filling dish.

8 oz (225 g) wholewheat spaghetti
2 tablespoons olive or other vegetable oil
1 medium onion, chopped
1 small cauliflower, cut into small florets and blanched in water for 2 minutes
4 tablespoons dry white wine
2 eggs, beaten
2 tablespoons grated Parmesan cheese
1–2 tablespoons fresh basil or tarragon or
½ tablespoon dried basil or tarragon
salt and freshly ground black pepper to taste

GARNISH
fresh basil sprig
4–5 green or black olives

Cook the spaghetti in lots of salted boiling water. Meanwhile heat the oil in a large pan. Sauté the onion until soft. Add the drained cauliflower and wine. Mix the eggs, cheese, basil or tarragon and seasoning together. Drain the spaghetti and toss it into the cauliflower. Carefully add the egg mixture, stirring all the time over a very gentle heat. Heat through until the egg scrambles. Garnish with a sprig of fresh basil and olives. Serve hot.

Noodles with Prawn and Lettuce Sauce

Serves 4

This is a good example of a demivegetarian recipe in which a wide variety of ingredients are combined in one dish. It is well flavoured, relatively low in saturated fats (depending on the oil used in the mayonnaise) and nutritious. It is at its best in the summertime when fresh broad beans and crisp lettuce are available.

4 oz (100 g) fine green noodles (fettucine) and 4 oz (100 g) wide yellow noodles (tagliatelle) or 8 oz (225 g) of just one variety
¼ pint (150 ml) thick natural yoghurt
¼ pint (150 ml) mayonnaise (see p. 15)
1 tablespoon chopped fresh dill or 1 teaspoon dried dill
4 oz (100 g) peeled prawns
4 oz (100 g) young broad beans, shelled and skinned (or use thawed frozen ones)
3 oz (75 g) finely shredded lettuce (iceberg is suitable)
salt and freshly ground black pepper to taste
4 oz (100 g) Parmesan cheese, grated

Cook the noodles in boiling salted water for 3−4 minutes (this is the cooking time for fresh pasta; if you are using dried pasta allow 8−10 minutes). Meanwhile put the yoghurt, mayonnaise, dill, prawns and broad beans into the top of a double saucepan and heat through gently. (Alternatively use a basin standing in a pan of gently simmering water.) Drain the cooked pasta thoroughly and toss together with the shredded lettuce. Spoon the pasta and lettuce into a warm bowl, add the prepared sauce and toss together. Season. Serve immediately with Parmesan cheese.

Tagliatelle with Courgette Sauce
Serves 4

1 large clove garlic, crushed
1 onion, peeled and chopped
3 sticks celery, chopped
8 oz (225 g) courgettes, topped, tailed and sliced
3 tablespoons vegetable oil
12 oz (350 g) fresh tomatoes, chopped
8 oz (225 g) wholewheat tagliatelle
salt and freshly ground black pepper to taste
3 oz (75 g) whole blanched almonds, toasted
4 oz (100 g) grated Parmesan cheese

Fry the garlic, onion, celery and courgettes gently in the oil for 10 minutes. Add the tomatoes and continue cooking until they have broken down into a pulp. Meanwhile cook the tagliatelle following the instructions on the packet. Drain well. Simmer the sauce for 5 minutes, then season with salt and black pepper. Pour the sauce over the tagliatelle, sprinkle almonds over the top and serve with Parmesan cheese.

Fried Celery and Toasted Almonds
Serves 4 as a side dish

An untrimmed head of celery weighs about 2¼ lb (1 kg) but most shops sell them trimmed of leaves. When buying a head of celery, choose one that has a thick, plump base and feels firm. The stems should not be too stringy or have brown, bruised patches. Healthy, fresh-looking leaves growing from the top of the stems are a good indication of quality, as is the overall even colour of each stem. To store celery, cut off the base, wash each stem, pat dry with a teatowel and keep in a cool place or in the salad drawer of the refrigerator for no more than two days. When washing celery, avoid soaking it in water for too long, as this has a softening effect (the Romans believed that hanging wreaths of crisp celery around the neck could protect a person from a hangover). Any outer stems that look damaged or rather coarse can be chopped and used for making stock or soup. The leaves are also full of flavour and they make a pretty garnish for meat, poultry and fish dishes. Celery can be braised, baked or stir-fried. Avoid fast boiling as celery needs slow cooking to break down its fibre, otherwise it will taste coarse and stringy and lack flavour. Celery is delicious made into soups or try it in this quick stir-fry recipe.

1 clove garlic, crushed
½ teaspoon ground cumin
4 tablespoons olive or other vegetable oil
6 sticks celery, washed and cut into
2 × ¼ in (2 × 6 mm) sticks
1 medium-sized red pepper, seeded and cut into thin strips
4 oz (100 g) French beans, topped, tailed and halved
1 tablespoon chopped fresh thyme or 1 teaspoon dried thyme
salt and black pepper to taste
1 oz (25 g) flaked almonds, toasted

In a deep frying pan or wok fry the garlic and cumin in the oil for 2–3 minutes until the garlic turns golden. Add the celery, red pepper and beans, and fry, stirring occasionally, for 8–10 minutes until the vegetables are almost soft but still have some texture. Add the thyme, salt and black pepper and half the flaked almonds. Stir for another minute and serve immediately with the remaining almonds scattered over the top.

Indian Summer Noodles
Serves 4

This recipe was sent to me by the Pasta Information Centre. It is a spicy dish using home-grown vegetables readily available in late summer and early autumn. (Black onion seeds can usually be obtained from Indian grocers). It makes a good one-pot vegetarian meal.

8 oz (225 g) wide noodles
1 tablespoon vegetable oil
2 oz (50 g) butter
2 cloves garlic, finely chopped
2 teaspoons ground coriander
1 lb (450 g) tomatoes, thinly sliced
2 teaspoons black onion seeds (optional)
¼–½ level teaspoon cayenne pepper
1 lb (450 g) courgettes, chopped into 1 in (2.5 cm) pieces
2 teaspoons soft brown sugar
1 bunch fresh coriander leaves

First break up the noodles so that they are in roughly 2 in (5 cm) lengths. Then cook them in boiling salted water until done. Drain the pasta and leave on one side in a bowl, stirring a little oil into it to stop the pieces sticking together. In a large deep frying pan or casserole heat the oil with 1 oz (25 g) butter over a medium heat. Add the garlic and ground coriander and stir for a minute. Then add the tomatoes, the onion seeds if used, the cayenne pepper and the courgettes, and stir over the heat for about 5 minutes until the courgettes are just cooked but still slightly crunchy. Now add the sugar, the remaining butter and the cooked noodles. Stir for another minute or so until the butter is melted. Remove the pan from the heat, stir in the coriander leaves, transfer the mixture to a heated serving dish and serve immediately.

Fresh Tomato Tart

Serves 4 – 6

When buying tomatoes, check that their skins are not broken, that they are firm to the touch and that they have a bright, even colour. As a general rule, buy firm tomatoes for salads and use soft, overripe ones for sauces. For a quick snack, soft tomatoes are delicious coarsely chopped and grilled and served on toast with a little ground black pepper. If you want to stuff and bake tomatoes, buy the larger firmer ones. Small cherry tomatoes are ideal for garnishes, for threading on skewers for kebabs or for adding to salads; they are especially popular with children because of their sweet flavour and small size. A good way of using up soft, overripe tomatoes is to make a raw tomato sauce, which can be prepared in advance and then either frozen or stored in the refrigerator for a few days (see p. 14). Or try them in one of the following tart recipes.

6 oz (175 g) wholewheat shortcrust pastry (see p. 17)
1 tablespoon olive oil
1½ lb (700 g) tomatoes, chopped
1 large clove garlic, peeled and crushed
salt and freshly ground black pepper to taste
3 tablespoons tomato purée
½ teaspoon grated orange rind
1 teaspoon chopped fresh mint
½ teaspoon brown sugar
3 oz (75 g) mozzarella cheese, thinly sliced

Preheat oven to 190°C (375°F, gas mark 5). Roll out the pastry thinly. Line an 8 in (20 cm) loose-bottomed flan tin. Press up the edges well and pinch neatly. Line with greaseproof paper and bake blind for 10 minutes. Meanwhile prepare the filling. Heat the oil in a large shallow pan. Add the tomatoes, garlic, salt and black pepper. Cook gently for 5 minutes. Add the tomato purée, orange rind, mint and sugar. Cook gently for 10 – 15 minutes until the sauce is thick and richly coloured. Spread the tomato mixture evenly in the pastry case. Top with the slivers of cheese. Return to the oven for 30 minutes. Serve warm, cut into wedges.

Tomato, Basil and Tuna Fish Tart

Serves 4–6

8 oz (225 g) wholewheat shortcrust pastry (see p. 17)
2 medium eggs
1 egg yolk
½ pint (275 ml) tomato sauce (see p. 14)
salt and freshly ground black pepper to taste
8 oz (225 g) canned tuna fish, flaked
1 lb (450 g) fresh tomatoes, skinned, seeded and chopped
2 tablespoons finely chopped basil or 2 teaspoons dried basil

Preheat oven to 190°C (375°F, gas mark 5). Roll out the pastry and use it to line a 9 in (22.5 cm) flan case. Set aside in the refrigerator. Beat together the eggs, egg yolk and tomato sauce and season with salt and black pepper. Stir in the tuna fish, tomatoes and basil. Pour the mixture into the pastry case and bake in the preheated oven for 30 minutes or until set. Serve hot or cold.

Note: To skin and deseed tomatoes, cut a few nicks in each one around the stalk end and plunge them into a bowl of boiling water for 40–60 seconds. Drain and rinse them under cold running water for a few minutes. The skins will now easily slide off. Cut the tomatoes in half lengthways and scoop the seeds out with a teaspoon.

Brussels Sprouts with Carrot and Cheese Sauce
Serves 4–6

Brussels sprouts are a hardy vegetable and need very little preparation. When buying Brussels sprouts, choose ones with healthy, bright green outer leaves with no discolouration. Store them in a cool dry place. Before cooking, cut a small cross in the stalk of each one – they will cook more evenly. Many people overcook sprouts by using too much water and cooking them for too long. Approximately 1 in (2.5 cm) water is sufficient. Alternatively they can be steamed in a steamer or in a covered metal colander over a pan of simmering water. Brussels sprouts have a delicious texture and flavour when used shredded raw in winter salads. They need quite a robust dressing, such as a mixture of olive oil, red wine vinegar, mustard, garlic, seasoning and a hard herb like rosemary or sage. Add a few onion rings or walnuts for extra texture. Shredded Brussels sprouts, stir-fried in olive oil with onion rings, broccoli florets, strips of red pepper and a pinch of cayenne pepper, make a delicious spicy dish which is quick and easy to prepare. Or try them in this more substantial vegetarian dish.

1 lb (450 g) Brussels sprouts
½ medium cauliflower, divided into florets
1 small can whole, peeled chestnuts, rinsed and drained
1 oz (25 g) vegetable margarine or butter
1 oz (25 g) plain flour
¾ pint (450 ml) skimmed milk
3 oz (75 g) cheese, grated
½ teaspoon dried mustard
salt and freshly ground black pepper to taste
3 medium carrots, peeled and grated

Preheat oven to 180°C (350°F, gas mark 4). Cook the sprouts and cauliflower in separate pans of boiling salted water (do not use too much water) until just tender but still crisp (*al dente*). Drain the vegetables, refresh them under cold water and drain again. Arrange the vegetables with the chestnuts in a greased ovenproof dish. Melt the margarine in a saucepan. Stir in the flour and cook for 30 seconds. Gradually add the milk, stirring continuously. Add the cheese, mustard, salt and black pepper, stirring continuously until the cheese is melted. Finally add the carrots and pour the sauce over the vegetables. Cook the dish in the preheated oven for 15 minutes until the top is golden brown.

Note: This dish can be assembled up to 8 hours in advance. Cover and keep in the refrigerator. Cook as above before serving.

STUFFED VEGETABLES

Stuffed vegetables are a speciality of Middle Eastern cuisine. Almost any vegetable available to the Middle Eastern cook is adapted in this way. Stuffings containing minced meat are common, but there are also rice, bulgar wheat, chicken and vegetable-based fillings. In the recipes given here peppers are stuffed with lentils and bulgar wheat, but lentils and rice or other beans or grains may be used. Variations using other vegetables and chicken stuffing are given below. The peppers or the vegetables may be cooked in a shallow bath of water or stock or, for a richer dish, in tomato sauce.

Vegetable-and-Tuna-Fish-Stuffed Vine Leaves
Serves 4

Vine leaves may be bought in tins or packets. To separate tangled leaves soak them for a couple of minutes in very hot water. Cut off any coarse stems.

7 oz (200 g) tin tuna fish, drained
2 hardboiled eggs, shelled and chopped
1 tablespoon chopped chives or spring onions
rind of 1/2 lemon, finely grated
1 clove garlic, crushed
3 oz (75 g) lettuce, finely shredded
2 courgettes, coarsely grated
2 tablespoons fresh wholemeal breadcrumbs
salt and freshly ground black pepper to taste
16 vine leaves, rinsed
1/2 pint (300 ml) tomato sauce (see p. 14)
2 teaspoons capers

Mix the tuna fish with the chopped hardboiled eggs, chives or spring onions, lemon rind, garlic, lettuce, courgettes, breadcrumbs and salt and black pepper. Divide the mixture into eight even-sized portions and shape each one into a small sausage. Wrap each portion in two vine leaves, neatly tucking in the ends. Place the parcels in a shallow pan, spoon the tomato sauce over them, add the capers and adjust the seasoning. Cover and simmer gently for about 40 minutes. Serve hot or chilled, allowing two stuffed vine leaves per person.

Peppers Stuffed with Lentils and Bulgar Wheat

Serves 4

4 large green or red peppers
4 tablespoons olive oil
1 medium onion, diced
1/2 teaspoon allspice
1/2 teaspoon ground cinnamon
1/2 teaspoon sugar
8 oz (225 g) cooked brown or green lentils
8 oz (225 g) bulgar wheat, washed and drained, or cooked white rice
2 tablespoons chopped fresh parsley
2 oz (50 g) walnuts, chopped
16 fl oz (450 ml) water, stock or tomato sauce (see p. 14)

Preheat oven to 180°C (350°F, gas mark 4). Cut the tops off the peppers and remove the pith and seeds. Reserve the tops. Put half the oil in a heavy saucepan and sauté the onion until soft. Add the allspice, cinnamon and sugar and stir well. Add the lentils and bulgar wheat or rice and sauté, stirring often, for 5 minutes. Pack this mixture into the peppers. Brush the peppers with some of the remaining oil and pack them tightly in a baking dish. Replace the tops and sprinkle them with the chopped walnuts and a little more olive oil. Add the water, stock or tomato sauce. Cover the dish with foil and bake in preheated oven for 30–35 minutes or until the peppers are tender.

GARNISH (OPTIONAL)
1/2 teaspoon salt
2 cloves garlic
1 teaspoon dried mint
juice of 1 lemon

In a pestle and mortar crush together the salt, garlic and mint. Stir in the lemon juice and sprinkle the mixture over the hot stuffed vegetables before serving.

VARIATIONS

Chicken filling: Follow the recipe as above but use the following spiced chicken stuffing in place of the lentils and bulgar wheat.

2 tablespoons olive oil
2 medium onions, finely diced
2 cloves garlic, crushed
1 lb (450 g) cooked chicken, minced
2 oz (50 g) pine nuts or whole blanched almonds
½ teaspoon allspice
1 teaspoon cinnamon
2 tablespoons freshly chopped parsley, mint or coriander
salt and black pepper to taste

Heat the oil in a frying pan and sauté the onions and garlic until golden. Add the chicken and pine nuts or almonds and brown gently. Add the remaining ingredients. Stir well and cook over a low heat for a further 5 minutes. Allow the filling to cool a little before stuffing the peppers.

Stuffed courgettes: Replace the peppers in the recipe above with courgettes. The filling is made in the same way (use the lentils and bulgar wheat or the chicken filling). To prepare the courgettes for stuffing, cut the stem ends off four large or eight small courgettes and carefully hollow out the centre of each with an apple corer, leaving an ⅛–¼ in (3–6 mm) shell. Soak the hollowed courgettes in salted water for 10 minutes then drain. Pack them with the filling and then arrange them in a heavy casserole. Add the water, stock or tomato sauce and bring the pot to the boil. Cover, reduce the heat and simmer for 30 minutes or until the courgettes are tender.

This recipe can also be adapted to suit a variety of stuffed vegetables such as marrows, tomatoes, onions, apples, fennel or vine or cabbage leaves.

Indian Vegetable Kichiri
Serves 4

The English breakfast dish kedgeree was derived from this Indian recipe in which lentils, brown rice and vegetables are cooked together in one pot.

2 tablespoons vegetable oil
1 medium onion, thinly sliced
1 medium carrot, grated
8 oz (225 g) long-grain brown rice, washed and drained
4 oz (100 g) green or brown lentils, soaked overnight and drained
2 tablespoons desiccated coconut, lightly dry-roasted
1 teaspoon cumin seeds
1 teaspoon powdered cinnamon
½ teaspoon ground turmeric
¼ teaspoon ground cloves
1 ½ pint (850 ml) boiling water
salt to taste

GARNISH
1 banana, sliced
2 oz (50 g) roasted almonds or peanuts

To dry-roast the coconut, heat it in a small dry frying pan over a moderate heat until it is just starting to brown. Heat the oil in a large pan and sauté the onion until just soft. Add the carrot and continue sautéeing until the onion is light brown in colour. Add the rice and lentils and fry over a low heat, stirring, for 5 minutes. Add the coconut and spices, mix well and cook, stirring for a further 2 minutes. Add the boiling water, mix and season with salt. Reduce the heat to as low as possible, cover the pan and simmer for 45−50 minutes or until all the liquid is absorbed and the rice and lentils are tender. Serve garnished with slices of banana and roasted almonds or peanuts.

Bean Enchiladas
Serves 4

Enchiladas are filled tortillas, which are Mexican flour or cornmeal pancakes or flat breads. The wheatflour variety are softer and more suitable for wrapping around fillings.

2 tablespoons vegetable oil
1 small onion, coarsely chopped
1/2 green pepper, cored, seeded and coarsely chopped
1 small dried chilli, seeded and finely chopped
1 clove garlic, crushed
1 lb (450 g) tinned red beans
8 fl oz (225 ml) tinned tomatoes, drained and chopped
1 teaspoon chilli powder
1/2 teaspoon ground cumin
salt and black pepper to taste
8 wheatflour tortillas (shop-bought)
1/4 head of lettuce, shredded
4 tomatoes, coarsely chopped
4 oz (100 g) Cheddar cheese, grated

Preheat oven to 180°C (350°F, gas mark 4). In a large saucepan heat the oil over a medium heat. Add the onion, pepper and dried chilli. Cook until tender. Add the garlic, beans, tinned tomatoes, chilli powder and cumin, and season with salt and pepper. Cover and simmer gently over a low heat for 10 minutes. Meanwhile place the tortillas on a baking sheet and bake them in the preheated oven for 5 minutes. Fill each tortilla shell with a portion of the bean mixture. Fold them up and place two on each plate. Top with lettuce, tomatoes and cheese. Serve immediately.

VEGETABLE BHAJIS

Bhajis are spicy Indian side dishes usually made with one or two vegetables and occasionally with more. They are eaten with rice, puris or chapattis and dal and/or a main meat or vegetarian dish.

Here is a selection of three vegetable bhaji dishes. Each serves four people as a side dish and may be prepared individually to accompany a main curry dish. Alternatively prepare all three of them and serve with chapattis, rice and cucumber in yoghurt for a simple Indian vegetarian meal.

Cauliflower Bhaji
Serves 4

3 oz (75 g) plus 1 tablespoon ghee or butter
1 medium potato, peeled and finely diced
1 teaspoon turmeric
½ teaspoon cumin seeds
1 in (2.5 cm) root ginger, very thinly sliced
½ teaspoon chilli powder (optional)
1 medium cauliflower, cut into equal-sized florets
salt and freshly ground black pepper to taste

In a heavy saucepan or casserole with a lid heat the ghee or butter and add the potato, turmeric, cumin, ginger and chilli if used. Sauté, stirring, for 2 minutes. Add the cauliflower and sauté over a low heat for 5 minutes. Season with salt. Cover the pan and cook over a gentle heat for 10–15 minutes until the cauliflower is tender. Serve sprinkled with freshly ground black pepper and dotted with butter.
Note: The potato may be omitted. It is included only to thicken up the sauce.
This recipe is also suitable for the preparation of bhindi bhaji (okra). Replace the cauliflower by 1 lb (450 g) young okra pods. If the pods are young and tender use them whole. Otherwise they will have to be sliced.

Spinach Bhaji
Serves 4

1½ lb (700 g) fresh spinach or 10 oz (300 g) frozen spinach, defrosted
2 oz (50 g) ghee or butter
1 medium onion, thinly sliced
2 cloves garlic, crushed
1 teaspoon cumin seeds
1 teaspoon turmeric powder
1–2 dry red chillies, crushed (optional)
1 in (2.5 cm) root ginger, grated
salt to taste

Pick over the spinach, remove any bad leaves and cut off any thick stalks. If the leaves are big, chop them coarsely, wash them well and drain. (This stage is omitted if you are using frozen spinach). Heat the ghee or butter in a large heavy saucepan or casserole with a lid and fry the onion and garlic until light brown, stirring all the time. Stir in the cumin and turmeric and then the chillies if used and ginger. Sauté for 1 minute. Add the spinach, cover and cook over a low to moderate heat for 8–10 minutes or until the spinach is wilted. Add the salt and cook, uncovered, until nearly all the liquid has gone. Cover the pot and cook for a further 5 minutes over a gentle heat.

If you dislike hot food, omit the chillies in this recipe.

Aubergine Bhaji
Serves 4

1 lb (450 g) aubergines, cut into ¾ in (2 cm) cubes
salt
4 oz (100 g) ghee or butter
4 cloves garlic, crushed
1 teaspoon turmeric powder
1 teaspoon cumin seeds
1–2 green chillies, finely chopped
1 in (2.5 cm) root ginger, grated
1 teaspoon garam masala (optional)

Sprinkle the aubergine cubes with salt, press them for 30 minutes, then rinse and drain them well. Heat the ghee or butter in a heavy saucepan or casserole and sauté the garlic until golden. Stir in the turmeric and cumin and mix well with the garlic and oil. Add the chillies, ginger and aubergines and stir well. Season with salt to taste. Cover and cook over a very low heat for 20 minutes. Remove the lid from the pan and cook uncovered until most of the moisture has evaporated and the aubergine is tender. If you wish add garam masala and heat through before serving.

Note: Slicing and salting aubergines before use draws off their slightly bitter juices; it also reduces the amount of oil that they absorb.

Lentil-Stuffed Apples

Serves 4

This dish is an unusual and nutritious combination of fruit, lentils and rice. It is a convenient way of using up leftover rice and lentils (or other combinations of pulses and grains). Serve it as the centrepiece of a main meal accompanied by a bowl of plain yoghurt, bulgar wheat and a green salad.

4 medium to large cooking apples, cored
4 fl oz (100 ml) water
2 tablespoons vegetable oil
1 medium onion, diced
4 oz (100 g) sultanas, soaked and drained
4 oz (100 g) cooked lentils, drained
4 oz (100 g) cooked rice, drained
1/2 teaspoon ground cumin
1/2 teaspoon turmeric
1/2 teaspoon salt
1/2 teaspoon black pepper
1 teaspoon sugar

Preheat the oven to 150°C (300°F, gas mark 2). Cut the tops off the apples and scoop out the pulp, leaving shells about ¼ in (6 mm) thick. Mix the pulp with the water and cook, covered, until tender. Remove the lid and simmer until the moisture has evaporated and the pulp is quite firm. Meanwhile, in the oil sauté the onion until golden. Combine half the pulp, the onion, half the sultanas and all the remaining ingredients except the sugar. Mix well and stuff the apples with the mixture. Combine the remaining pulp and sultanas with the sugar and spread the mixture on the base of a lightly buttered baking dish. Pack the stuffed apples on top and bake for 45 minutes.

Fried Celery and Toasted Almonds (page 68)

Poussins with Stilton Cream Cheese (page 91)

CHEESE, YOUGHURT AND CREAM

Dairy products in the demiveg diet are an important source of protein, minerals, especially calcium, the vitamins A and D and B vitamins, especially riboflavin (vitamin B2). With the exception of low-fat cheeses and yoghurt and skimmed milks, dairy products are also a source of saturated fats and should therefore be eaten in moderation as part of a mixed diet. This rule also applies to butter and to any margarine spreads. Spreads made from vegetable oils are normally higher in polyunsaturated fats, but butter is a natural product without additives and it is better to use this than either hardened margarines or some of the newly promoted soft spreads made from synthetically produced fats.

Cheese

Cheese is a useful ingredient to the cook. It is tasty and versatile and good in either cooked dishes or uncooked. There are many varieties of hard and soft cheeses, each with its own individual flavour and texture. When cooking with cheese choose a variety that is appropriate to the dish being prepared; in the recipes that follow I suggest particular types of cheese to use. Avoid overcooking cheese or it becomes tough and stringy.

TRADITIONAL HARD CHEESES
At one time in the British Isles there were numerous local cheeses but over the years the selection has dwindled and nowadays there are nine traditional regional cheeses commonly available. Fortunately, in the last few years this trend has been reversed and an increasing number of specialized British cheeses are appearing in the shops every year. Look for them at your local cheese counter or delicatessen and try them. The bigger the market the more incentive there is for cheesemakers to venture into new varieties. Some of the larger manufacturers are also producing low-fat hard cheeses such as Tendale, a Cheddar- or Cheshire-like variety. These cheeses make good low-fat sauces and fillings for flans and quiches.

ENGLISH CHEDDAR
Cheddar was first recorded as being made in Somerset in the early sixteenth century and now is copied the world over. It is a rich, nutty-tasting cheese with a close, creamy texture. A red variety is also available, coloured with annatto, a natural vegetable dye obtained from the seed-pods of a South American shrub.

CAERPHILLY
This cheese was first made in the Welsh village of Caerphilly in Glamorgan. It is a moist, crumbly white cheese with a mild, slightly salty flavour. It is especially good with celery and slices of bread and butter.

CHESHIRE

This is the oldest of all the English cheeses and is mentioned in the Domesday Book. The natural salt in the soil gives the cheese its tangy flavour. It is a loose, crumbly cheese and is delightful eaten with fruit, cake and biscuits. There are red, white and blue varieties of Cheshire.

DERBY

Derby cheese is similar in texture to Cheddar but is moister and has a more delicate flavour. When young it is mild in taste and pale honey in colour; as it matures it develops a fuller flavour and darker colour. Sometimes Derby is flavoured with sage leaves to create Sage Derby. It is excellent eaten with fruit, particularly pears and apples, and a perfect ingredient for a ploughman's lunch.

DOUBLE GLOUCESTER

Originally made from the rich milk of Gloucestershire cattle, there used to be a single as well as a double Gloucester, both shaped like a millstone, but one, as its name implies, was larger than the other. It is a golden-coloured cheese with a smooth, close texture and a rich, mellow flavour, and is particularly good with salad or fresh fruit.

LANCASHIRE

Until comparatively recently Lancashire cheese was not well-known outside its own county. It is a crumbly white cheese with a creamy mild taste which grows stronger as the cheese matures. This cheese is especially good as a topping on soups and for toasting.

LEICESTER

This cheese originated in the region around Melton Mowbray and is one of the most easily identifiable of the traditional cheeses because of its bright reddish colour. This comes from the addition of annatto. It has a higher moisture content than Cheddar, an open, granular texture and a clean, fresh flavour.

STILTON

Stilton is one of our most famous cheeses and has been produced in the Vale of Belvoir and the Dove Valley for generations. Today it is still made only in Leicestershire, Nottinghamshire and Derbyshire. There are two types of Stilton – blue and white. Blue Stilton is the best known. The blue veining is made by piercing holes in the cheeses during the ripening process to allow air to penetrate and produce the blue mould. White Stilton is moist, young cheese sold after four weeks' maturing before the blue veins can develop. Stilton is the perfect end to a meal.

WENSLEYDALE

This cheese, originally made from ewes' milk, was brought to this country at the time of the Norman Conquest and first produced by the monks of Jervaulx Abbey in the Yorkshire Dales. It is a white cheese, with a mild, creamy, sweet taste and a flaky texture. It is delicious accompanied by an apple or apple pie. A blue variety of Wensleydale is also available.

SOFT CHEESES

Soft cheeses are those which do not involve pressing during preparation. They do not keep as well as hard cheeses and should be bought as needed. Soft cheeses are used in savoury recipes and also in sweet dishes such as cheesecake, fruit flans and pies. Cottage cheese is perhaps our best-known soft cheese. It is prepared from skimmed milk and is very low in fat. In Britain soft cheeses are categorized by their fat content and they are divided into six grades, ranging from skimmed-milk soft cheese with a fat content of less than 1 per cent to double cream cheeses with over 65 per cent fat.

STORING AND SERVING CHEESE

Cheese should be stored at between 5°C (40°F) and 10°C (50°F) which is fortunately the temperature range of the main compartment of the average domestic refrigerator. It should be stored wrapped in cling film or in a closed container to prevent it picking up the odours of other foods. Cheese can also be stored in a cool larder if the temperature remains below 10°C (50°F). Most cheeses do not freeze satisfactorily. Freezing adversely affects the taste and texture. The exception to this rule is grated cheese and most medium- to full-fat curd and cream cheeses.

Yoghurt

Yoghurt is an excellent food. Like the milk from which it is made, it is low to medium in fat and an excellent source of protein, vitamins and minerals, especially calcium. It is easily digested and a versatile ingredient. Yoghurt also has the claimed reputation of prolonging longevity and as a source of stamina. It may be used in the preparation of soups and salads as a marinating agent, in main meals and in desserts, and even as a summer drink mixed with water, a pinch of salt and mint. Other ideas are as follows:–

Add chopped fruit, such as apple or banana, to a carton of plain or fruit yoghurt.
Stir half a carton of your favourite fruit yoghurt into a glass of cold milk to make a refreshing drink.
Blend equal amounts of plain yoghurt and fruit purée together for a quick fruit fool.
Stir a carton of plain yoghurt into a chicken casserole to give the sauce some bite.
Make up half a jelly with water according to packet directions, stir or whisk in a carton of fruit or plain yoghurt and allow to set.

Mix plain yoghurt with mayonnaise to give a lighter salad dressing.

Dairy Creams

Dairy creams are delicious in savoury and sweet dishes but they are rich in saturated fats and should be used in moderation. In cooked dishes use single rather than double cream or, where appropriate, use a low-fat standby such as yoghurt, curd cheese or cottage cheese. The latter alternatives may also be used in desserts. There is also a growing number of British and imported low-fat dairy products available for use as substitutes for cream. Two newly popular products are *fromage frais*, made from fermented skimmed milk, and *crème fraîche*, made from double cream and low-fat yoghurt or sour cream. *Fromage frais* is used as an alternative to whipping cream and *crème fraîche* in the traditional French manner as an accompaniment to fresh fruit desserts.

FLANS AND QUICHES

Courgette and Tomato Cheese Flan
Serves 6

A simple and convenient dish to make for lunch or a light dinner. If fresh herbs are available they will lift its flavour to something special. For the occasional treat replace the milk with single cream.

10 oz (275 g) wholewheat shortcrust pastry (see p. 17)
8 oz (225 g) courgettes
1 oz (25 g) butter
2 cloves garlic, crushed
4 tomatoes, skinned and thinly sliced
2 eggs
¼ pint (150 ml) milk or single cream
3 oz (75 g) English Cheddar cheese, grated
salt and freshly ground black pepper to taste
2 teaspoons fresh basil or ½ teaspoon dried basil
2 teaspoons fresh oregano or ½ teaspoon dried oregano

Roll out the pastry on a floured surface and use it to line a 9 in (22.5 cm) flan dish or ring. Prick the base and chill until required. Preheat oven to 190°C (375°F, gas mark 5). Wash and slice the courgettes. Melt the butter in a pan, add the courgettes and garlic and cook for a few minutes until they begin to soften. Arrange the tomato slices and courgettes in the flan case. Beat together the eggs, milk or cream and cheese. Add the seasoning, oregano and basil and pour the mixture over the courgettes and tomatoes. Bake in the preheated oven for 40–45 minutes or until the filling is set and golden brown on top. Serve hot or cold.

Avocado and Chicken Flan

Serves 4–6

Avocados can be used in both savoury and sweet dishes and, to be enjoyed to the full, they must be eaten when fully ripe. If you buy an underripe avocado, wrap it in a brown paper bag or newspaper and leave it in a warm place, such as an airing cupboard, until it ripens. Firmer avocados can be used in cooked dishes. Cut avocado browns very quickly, so once you have sliced or halved an avocado, brush the cut surface with lemon juice.

One way of using up an overripe avocado is to turn it into a dip. Mash the avocado flesh and mix it with natural yoghurt, a little mayonnaise, Worcestershire sauce, crushed garlic, seasoning and chopped spring onion. Serve with sticks of raw crisp vegetables.

Avocado and potato purée makes a delicious accompanying vegetable. Mix mashed avocado flesh with puréed cooked potato and season with salt, pepper and ground nutmeg.

For a more substantial dish try this recipe for avocado and chicken flan.

6 oz (175 g) wholemeal shortcrust pastry (see p. 17)
3 spring onions, chopped
1 firmish avocado, halved, peeled and chopped into ½ in (1 cm) cubes
4 oz (100 g) cooked chicken, cut into thin strips
2 eggs
¼ pint (150 ml) natural yoghurt
¼ pint (150 ml) fresh or skimmed milk
2 tablespoons finely chopped parsley
salt, freshly ground black pepper and ground nutmeg to taste

Preheat the oven to 190°C (375°F, gas mark 5). Line a 9 in (22.5 cm) flan case with the pastry and bake blind in the oven for about 8 minutes. Line the case with the spring onions, avocado and chicken. Beat together the eggs, yoghurt, milk, parsley, salt, black pepper and nutmeg. Pour the mixture into the case and bake for 30 minutes or until set and a light golden colour.

Lettuce and Smoked Haddock Quiche
Serves 6

This protein-rich but low-fat demivegetarian recipe uses fish, eggs, yoghurt and lettuce to make an unusual but very tasty quiche.

8 oz (225 g) wholewheat shortcrust pastry (see p. 17)
12 oz (350 g) smoked haddock, lightly poached and flaked
4 oz (100 g) finely shredded iceberg lettuce and 2 oz (50 g) chopped iceberg lettuce
2 spring onions, finely chopped
1 teaspoon fresh dill
1 hardboiled egg, shelled and finely chopped
3 eggs
8 oz (225 g) thick Greek yoghurt
1 clove garlic, peeled
salt and freshly ground black pepper

Preheat oven to 190°C (375°F, gas mark 5). Roll out the pastry and use it to line a flan dish or ring 9 in (22.5 cm) in diameter. Press up the edges well. Mix the flaked haddock with the shredded lettuce, spring onions, dill and hardboiled egg and arrange the mixture in the pastry case. Put the chopped lettuce, eggs, yoghurt, garlic and salt and pepper in a liquidizer or food processor and blend until smooth. Pour the yoghurt and egg mixture into the pastry case. Bake in the preheated oven for about 35 minutes until well risen; the filling should be golden and just set. Serve warm.

Gower Flan
Serves 4–6

This delicious Welsh recipe makes use of Welsh coastal produce such as laver seaweed (it is worth trying to obtain this, but if it is unavailable spinach may be used instead), cockles and prawns. To give it the finishing touch Caerphilly cheese is recommended although another cheese such as Cheddar could be used.

8 oz (225 g) wholewheat shortcrust pastry (see p. 17)
½ oz (15 g) flour
1 ½ oz (40 g) butter
¼ pint (150 ml) milk
2 fl oz (50 ml) dry white wine
3 fl oz (75 ml) single cream
salt and pepper to taste
1 oz (25 g) shelled prawns and 4 unshelled prawns
6 oz (125 g) laverbread or thawed frozen spinach, chopped
10 oz (275 g) cockles in brine, drained
4 oz (100 g) Caerphilly cheese, grated
8 small croutons

Preheat oven to 190°C (375°F, gas mark 5). On a lightly floured worktop roll out the pastry and use it to line a 9 in (22.5 cm) flan dish. Prick the base and bake blind in the preheated oven for 10 minutes. Place the flour, butter and milk in a saucepan and heat, stirring continuously, until the sauce thickens and boils. It should have a smooth consistency. Stir in the white wine, single cream and seasoning. Reheat gently and add the shelled prawns. Spread a good layer of laverbread or spinach (reserving some for the garnish) over the base of the flan and arrange the cockles on top, reserving eight for garnishing. Pour the sauce over the top and sprinkle it with cheese. Bake for 15 minutes until golden brown. Spread a little of the remaining laverbread or spinach on each crouton and top with a reserved cockle. Use them together with the unshelled prawns to garnish the flan. The croutons and prawns can be dipped in a little aspic if desired and allowed to set firm before garnishing.

Crabmeat and Cottage Cheese Quiche

Serves 6

This recipe makes six small individual quiches which are excellent for a luncheon or in a picnic. Frozen crabmeat is convenient and economical to buy but, if you prefer, fresh crabmeat may be used instead.

10 oz (275 g) wholewheat shortcrust pastry (see p. 17)
1 lb (450 g) crabmeat, combine brown and white meat
2 teaspoons lemon juice
cayenne, salt and black pepper to taste
3 fl oz (75 ml) milk
2 eggs
8 oz (225 g) cottage cheese (flavoured with chives if preferred)

Preheat oven to 190°C (375°F, gas mark 5). Roll out the pastry and use it to line six 4 in (10 cm) individual quiche dishes. Prick the bases with a fork. Mix together the crabmeat, lemon juice and cayenne, salt and black pepper. Spoon equal portions of this mixture into the quiche cases. Beat the milk and eggs together, mix in the cottage cheese and season with salt and black pepper. Divide the mixture equally between the crabmeat-filled cases. Place them on a baking sheet and bake in the preheated oven for 40 minutes. Allow the quiches to cool a little and then remove them from their dishes. Serve hot or cold.

Note: The quiches should not be deep-frozen if frozen crabmeat was used in their preparation.

Derbyshire Quiche
Serves 4

This quiche is made with sage Derby cheese and it has the same mild but distinctive herb flavour. Incidentally, sage is said to aid the digestion.

6 oz (175 g) wholewheat shortcrust pastry (see p. 17)
1 lb (450 g) onions, finely chopped
1 tablespoon vegetable oil
1 oz (25 g) butter
2 eggs, beaten
2 tablespoons single cream or milk
1 teaspoon prepared mustard (tarragon mustard if available)
salt and black pepper to taste
4 oz (100 g) Sage Derby cheese, grated

Preheat oven to 190°C (375°F, gas mark 5). On a lightly floured work surface roll out the pastry and use it to line an 8 in (20.5 cm) flan ring or dish. Prick the base and bake blind for 10 minutes. Sauté the onions in the oil and butter until softened. Spread them over the base of the pastry case. Combine the eggs, cream and milk, mustard and salt and black pepper and pour the mixture over the onions. Sprinkle the cheese over the top and bake for 30 minutes or until the filling is set and the top gently browned.

Potato, Cheese and Onion Pie
Serves 4

A tasty, low-fat demiveg version of an old favourite.

1 medium onion, thinly sliced
1 tablespoon vegetable oil
3 large potatoes, cooked in their skins for about 10 minutes and then peeled and thinly sliced
2 leeks, cut into rings and parboiled
4 oz (100 g) curd cheese
2 tablespoons chopped chives
6 tomatoes, seeded and chopped
1 clove garlic, peeled and chopped
salt and pepper to taste
4 tablespoons chicken stock or water
2 tablespoons grated Parmesan cheese

Preheat oven to 190°C (375°F, gas mark 5). Fry the onion gently in the oil. Place layers of onion, potato and leeks in an ovenproof dish with small knobs of curd cheese between each layer. Mix together the chives, tomatoes, garlic, salt and pepper and chicken stock or water. Spoon the mixture over the vegetable layers and sprinkle the top with Parmesan cheese. Bake in the preheated oven for 25 minutes.

Poussins with Stilton Cream Cheese

Makes 4 large or 8 small portions

Poussins are young chickens from four to eight weeks old. They should weigh about 1 lb (0.5 kg) and provide one large or two small portions. This dish is perfect for a special occasion. The sauce is rich and thus best served with a simple salad and lightly boiled vegetables.

4 poussins
salt and black pepper to taste
4 oz (100 g) butter or polyunsaturated margarine
8 oz (225 g) mushrooms, sliced
4 tablespoons brandy
10 fl oz (300 ml) fresh single cream
4 oz (100 g) blue Stilton cheese
parsley sprigs to garnish

Preheat the oven to 200°C (400°F, gas mark 6). Carefully wash the poussins, pat them dry and season with salt and black pepper. Dot each bird with a little butter (use about half the butter). Place them in the oven and roast them for 1 hour. Melt the remaining butter in a heavy saucepan and sauté the mushrooms for about 5 minutes. Reduce the heat to very low and add the brandy. Stir and leave the mushrooms to marinate over a low heat for 15 minutes. Increase the heat a little and add the cream. Stir continuously until it thickens. Crumble the Stilton into the sauce and stir until it melts. Arrange the poussins on individual dishes, pour some sauce over each and garnish with a sprig or two of parsley. Serve the remainder of the sauce in a jug.

Cheese, Pasta and Vegetable Bake
Serves 4

A simple but tasty and nutritious dish, and a good way of using up leftover cooked pasta.

8 oz (225 g) carrots, thickly sliced
8 oz (225 g) celery, coarsely chopped (reserve the leaves for garnish)
8 oz (225 g) cooked wholewheat pasta
3 tomatoes, sliced
1 oz (25 g) butter or polyunsaturated margarine
1 oz (25 g) plain flour
½ pint (275 ml) milk
salt and cayenne pepper to taste
1 teaspoon prepared mustard
6 oz (175 g) Cheddar cheese, grated

Preheat the oven to 190°C (375°F, gas mark 5). Grease a 2 pint (1 litre) ovenproof casserole dish with a little oil. Simmer the carrots and celery in a pan of boiling water until only just tender. Drain well and rinse them under cold water. Drain again. Combine the pasta and vegetables and spread a layer of half the mixture in the casserole dish. Cover this with the tomato slices, reserving three slices for use as a garnish. Cover the tomatoes with the remaining vegetable and pasta mixture. Melt the butter or margarine in a small, heavy saucepan, stir in the flour and cook for 1 minute. Slowly stir in the milk and bring to the boil. Stir continuously until the sauce just boils and thickens. Add the salt and cayenne pepper and stir in the mustard and most of the cheese. Pour the sauce over the pasta and vegetables. Sprinkle the remaining cheese over the top and bake in the preheated oven for 30 minutes. Serve garnished with reserved tomato slices and celery leaves.

VARIATION

This dish is also good with leeks and parsnips. The Cheddar cheese may be replaced with Red Leicester.

Derby Cheese and Spiced Fish
Serves 4

In this healthy mix of fish, cheese, vegetables and nuts, strips of cod fillet are simmered in a spiced yoghurt sauce, sprinkled with grated Derby cheese, surrounded with creamed potatoes and then grilled golden brown.

1 lb (450 g) cod fillets, skinned and cut into 2 in (5 cm) strips
2 level teaspoons turmeric
3 tablespoons vegetable oil
2 in (5 cm) cinnamon stick
2 medium onions, chopped
½ level teaspoon hot chilli powder
2 sticks celery, chopped
2 carrots, peeled and chopped
5 fl oz (150 ml) natural yoghurt
4 tablespoons water
2 oz (50 g) mixed nuts, chopped
salt and pepper to taste
4 oz (100 g) Derby cheese, grated
1 lb (450 g) potatoes, cooked and creamed

Sprinkle the fish strips with the turmeric. Heat the oil in a frying pan and fry the fish for 3–4 minutes, turning once. Lift the fish out of the pan and set aside on a dish. Add the cinnamon stick and onions to the pan and fry until the onions are lightly browned. Add the chilli powder, celery and carrots and fry gently for 10 minutes, stirring now and again. Stir in the yoghurt a tablespoon at a time, then add the water, the mixed nuts, salt and pepper and the fish pieces. Simmer gently for 5–10 minutes until the fish is tender. Transfer the mixture to an ovenproof casserole dish and sprinkle with half the cheese. Stir the remaining cheese into the potatoes and then pipe them around the edge of the dish. Grill until golden brown and serve immediately.

Cheese and Oat Burgers
Makes 4 burgers

A demiveg alternative to hamburgers, cheese and oat burgers are popular with children. Serve them in a wholemeal bun with a salad for lunch.

6 oz (175 g) Red Leicester cheese, grated
1 small green pepper, seeded and finely chopped
1 large tomato, skinned and finely chopped
1 small onion, finely chopped
4 oz (100 g) porridge oats
2 eggs
salt and freshly ground black pepper to taste
2–4 tablespoons vegetable oil

Reserve 2 oz (50 g) cheese for topping. Mix the remaining cheese with the pepper, tomato, onion and oats. Add the eggs and mix thoroughly until well blended. Season generously with salt and black pepper. If the mixture is a little sticky add more oats so that it binds together well. Divide the mixture into four portions and shape each into a burger. Heat about 2 tablespoons oil in a frying pan and gently fry the burgers until golden brown. Turn them carefully with a large spatula and continue cooking until golden brown on the second side. Add a little more oil if necessary. Sprinkle the reserved cheese over the burgers and place them under a hot grill until the tops are golden brown.

Cheese, Anchovy and Potato Layers
Serves 4

This dish is put together very quickly from simple ingredients but it tastes exceptionally good.

1 lb (450 g) potatoes, peeled and thinly sliced
1 large onion, thinly sliced
4 oz (100 g) tin anchovies
8 oz (225 g) cottage cheese
½ pint (275 ml) milk
salt and black pepper to taste

Preheat the oven to 190°C (375°F, gas mark 5). Butter an ovenproof dish and make a layer of half the potatoes in the bottom. Cover these with the onion rings and then distribute the anchovies evenly over the top. Cover the dish with the remaining potatoes. Mix together the cottage cheese, milk, salt and pepper and pour the mixture over the potatoes. Bake for 1 hour or until the potatoes are tender and browned on top.

Apple Fondue
Serves 4 — 6

Fondue, a cheese dish from Switzerland, is basically flavoured cheese melted in a pan which is then served at the table over a small spirit lamp or fondue burner. Guests eat the fondue by dipping pieces of French bread, vegetables and, in this case, apple slices into the melted cheese. Fondue is ideal for informal entertaining.

1 small garlic clove, skinned and halved
3/4 pint (450 ml) apple juice
1 level tablespoon cornflour
1/4 level teaspoon dry mustard
1/4 level teaspoon paprika
1 1/2 lb (700 g) Cheddar or Lancashire cheese, grated
4 — 6 dessert apples, peeled and cubed, or celery sticks and cauliflower florets or French bread, cubed

Rub the inside of a heavy fondue pan with the cut side of each half of the garlic clove. In a separate bowl mix a little apple juice with the cornflour, mustard and paprika to form a smooth consistency. Warm the remaining apple juice in the fondue pan. Gradually add the cheese, stirring continuously over a low heat until it has melted. Stir in the cornflour mixture and bring gently to the boil and continue stirring off the heat for a further minute until the fondue is smooth. Do not overcook otherwise the mixture will separate. Transfer the pan to a spirit lamp or fondue burner on a large table mat on the dining table. Serve cubes of dessert apples tossed in lemon juice, or pieces of celery and cauliflower florets, or cubes of French bread to dip in the hot cheese sauce. Warn your guests that the cheese fondue is very hot.

Lettuce, Basil and Cheese Roulade

Serves 6

Roulade is a French cooking term meaning something rolled up; traditionally a roulade is a thin strip of meat wrapped around a stuffing. Nowadays, as in this recipe, a roulade is more often made from a light savoury sponge base wrapped around a cheese-flavoured filling.

Fresh basil, especially the Greek variety that is so reminiscent of holidays on Greek islands, a crisp iceberg lettuce and a good Red Leicester cheese make this roulade a special treat. Serve with a salad.

1½ oz (40 g) margarine or butter
1½ oz (40 g) plain flour
¾ pint (450 ml) milk
salt and freshly ground black pepper to taste
3 eggs, separated
2 tablespoons chopped fresh basil
3 oz (175 g) iceberg lettuce, finely shredded
4 tablespoons mayonnaise
4 oz (100 g) Red Leicester cheese, coarsely grated
1 tablespoon mango chutney

Preheat the oven to 190°C (375°F, gas mark 5). Grease a large swiss-roll tin, approximately 12 × 8 in (30 × 20 cm) in size, and line it with baking parchment or buttered greaseproof paper. Melt the margarine or butter in a saucepan and then add the flour, stirring well. Cook for 30 seconds. Gradually add the milk and bring the mixture to the boil, stirring, until the sauce has thickened. Season with salt and black pepper. Beat in the egg yolks, half the chopped basil and the shredded lettuce. Whisk the egg whites until they are stiff but not dry and then fold them lightly but thoroughly into the sauce mixture. Spoon the prepared mixture into the lined tin and spread it out evenly. Bake in the preheated oven for about 15 minutes, until it is pale gold in colour. It should be just set, but still spongy to the touch. For the filling, mix the mayonnaise with the remaining chopped basil and the grated cheese, and add the chutney.

To serve hot, quickly turn the freshly baked roulade onto a sheet of greaseproof paper and remove the lining paper. Spread the sponge with the prepared filling and roll it up immediately, as for a swiss roll.

To serve cold, turn the cooked roulade onto a sheet of greaseproof paper and cover it with a damp teatowel. Once it is cool, remove the teatowel and lining paper, spread the filling on the sponge and roll it up. Serve cut in slices, with or without a sauce. Garnish with sprigs of basil.

Lettuce, Basil and Cheese Roulade (opposite page)

Skate with Courgette and Capers (page 124)

Tomato, Watercress and Cheese Roulade
Serves 4

In this second roulade recipe the sponge wrap is flavoured with fresh tomato. The filling is a light mustard-flavoured spread of cheese and watercress. Serve with a selection of green vegetables.

½ oz (12.5 g) butter or margarine
1 lb (450 g) tomatoes, skinned and finely chopped
1 oz (25 g) wholemeal flour
salt and freshly ground black pepper to taste
3 eggs, separated
1 egg white
3 oz (75 g) Cheddar cheese, grated
2 tablespoons chutney
½ teaspoon made mustard
3 tablespoons chopped watercress

Preheat the oven to 190°C (375°F, gas mark 5). Lightly grease a swiss roll tin, approximately 12 × 8 in (30 × 20 cm) in size, and line it with baking parchment or lightly buttered greaseproof paper. Melt the butter in a pan, add the tomatoes and cook for about 4 minutes until they are pulpy. Stir in the flour and cook over a gentle heat for 1 minute. Remove the pan from the heat, add the seasoning and beat in the egg yolks. Whisk the egg whites until they are stiff but not dry, and then fold them lightly but thoroughly into the tomato mixture. Spread the mixture evenly in the prepared tin, making sure that it reaches right to the edges. Bake in the preheated oven for about 20 minutes until the sponge is just set and firm to the touch. Meanwhile make the filling. Mix threequarters of the grated cheese with the chutney, mustard, half the watercress and salt and pepper. Quickly turn the cooked roulade out onto a clean sheet of baking parchment. Remove the lining paper. Spread the filling evenly over the roulade and roll up swiss-roll fashion. Place the roulade on an ovenproof serving dish and sprinkle it with the remaining watercress and cheese. Return it to the oven for 2–3 minutes. Serve cut into slices.

Cheese-Filled Triangle Fila Pastries
Serves 6−8

Fila pastry is very versatile and most useful for making different shaped pastries and pies. How to use fila pastry is described on p. 00. In the Middle East the most popular shape for savoury fila pastries is a small triangle. In this recipe we show how to make them and give three variations on cheese fillings. They may be served hot or cold as a hors d' oeuvre *(mezze)* or as part of a main course perhaps accompanied by a sauce. The recipe makes about 48 pastries − probably more than you will need at any one time − but they keep well and freeze well.

8 oz (225 g) fila pastry (about 12 sheets)
2 oz (50 g) melted butter

SIMPLE CHEESE FILLING
1 lb (450 g) Cheddar, Gruyère or feta cheese, grated
2 eggs, beaten
1 small bunch parsley, finely chopped
salt and black pepper to taste

Combine the ingredients and mix well.

MUSHROOM AND CHEESE FILLING
2 teaspoons olive oil
1 medium-sized onion
1 clove garlic, crushed
6 oz (175 g) mushrooms, finely sliced
1 teaspoon dried mixed herbs
¼ teaspoon cayenne pepper
1 hardboiled egg
8 oz (225 g) Cheddar or (for a stronger flavour) Parmesan cheese, grated
salt and black pepper to taste

Heat the oil in a frying pan and cook the onion and garlic for 3−4 minutes. Add the mushrooms, herbs and cayenne pepper. Cover and cook the mixture over a gentle heat for 10 minutes, then remove the pan from the heat. Shell the egg and chop the white coarsely. Mash the yolk into the mushroom mixture. Stir in the egg white, grated cheese and salt and pepper. Set aside to cool completely.

SPINACH AND CHEESE FILLING
1 lb (450 g) fresh spinach, washed
2 teaspoons olive oil
2 oz (50 g) cottage cheese
2 oz (50 g) Gruyère or Emmenthal cheese, grated
2 tablespoons thick yoghurt
1 egg
¼ teaspoon grated nutmeg
salt and black pepper to taste

Put the spinach into a pan, cover and cook in the water left on the leaves after washing until completely wilted (about 6 minutes). Drain, press dry and chop finely. Add the other ingredients to the spinach and gently beat them together.

FILLING AND BAKING THE PASTRIES

Preheat the oven to 200°C (400°F, gas mark 6). Cut one sheet of pastry into four strips 3 in (7.5 cm) wide. Fold up three of the strips and wrap them loosely in a teatowel for later use. Brush the remaining strip with butter and put a heaped teaspoon of the filling just inside the lower left edge of the pastry. Fold the bottom corner over the stuffing to meet the diagonally opposite corner and form a triangle. Continue folding the triangle over and over until the whole pastry strip has been used up. Place the filled pastry, seam side down, on a buttered baking tray. Repeat the procedure with the remaining three strips and then with the rest of the fila sheets, keeping them covered as you work. Brush all the pastries with melted butter and bake for 35 minutes or until the pastry is golden brown. Remove from baking tray and serve hot or cold.

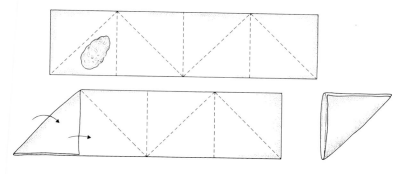

Quick Pizza Sandwich

Serves 1

1 pitta bread
tomatoes, sliced
cheese, grated
salt and freshly ground black pepper
(quantities according to taste)
olives
oregano

Preheat the oven to 230°C (450°F, gas mark 8). Cut the pitta bread around its circumference so that you can open it up as two orals joined by a hinge of bread. On one side make a layer of tomato slices, cover these with grated cheese and season with salt and black pepper. Decorate the layered side with olives and sprinkle it with oregano, and then fold the empty half of the bread over the top. Bake the pizza sandwich in the hot oven for 5 minutes or until the cheese has melted.

Wholemeal Pizza
Serves 4

Pizza is an excellent demivegetarian food. It combines complementary ingredients – the grains in the flour, the vegetables in the sauce and the various protein groups such as cheese, fish or chicken in the topping. It is particularly convenient to make if you bake your own bread as you can use some of your bread dough for the base.

DOUGH
¼ oz (7 g) fresh yeast
1 teaspoon brown sugar
5 fl oz (150 ml) lukewarm water
4 oz (100 g) wholemeal flour
1 teaspoon salt
1 tablespoon vegetable oil

PIZZA SAUCE
2 tablespoons olive oil
1 lb (450 g) ripe tomatoes, peeled and chopped,
or 14 oz (400 g) tin peeled tomatoes, chopped
2 tablespoons tomato purée
2 teaspoons chopped fresh oregano, or 1 teaspoon dried oregano
salt and pepper

PIZZA TOPPING
1 medium onion, thinly sliced
2 oz (50 g) mushrooms, sliced
1 medium green pepper, cored, seeded and thinly sliced
8 oz (225 g) Cheddar cheese, grated
anchovies (optional)
tuna fish, shredded (optional)
cooked chicken, shredded (optional)

TO MAKE THE DOUGH

Cream the yeast and sugar together, add the warm water and set aside in a warm place for 15–20 minutes or until the mixture has frothed up. Combine the flour, salt and oil in a mixing bowl, add the yeast mixture and mix into a fairly soft dough which easily comes away from the sides of the bowl. Remove the dough from the bowl and knead on a floured surface for 5 minutes until it is smooth and elastic. Alternatively, place the flour, salt and oil in the bowl of a food processor and, with the machine running, pour the yeast liquid through the feed tube. Blend until the mixture forms a ball around the knife and then blend for another 15–20 seconds to knead the dough. Place the dough in a clean bowl and cover with a damp cloth; leave it in a warm place for 45 minutes–1 hour.

TO MAKE THE PIZZA SAUCE

Heat the oil in a saucepan, add the tomatoes, tomato purée, half the oregano, salt

100

and pepper. Cook over a low heat, stirring occasionally for 15 minutes or until the excess liquid has evaporated and a thick purée remains. Set aside to cool.

TO MAKE THE PIZZA

Preheat the oven to 240°C (475°F, gas mark 9). Punch down the dough with your fists and knead it lightly until it is smooth again. Grease the base of a pizza tray or flan ring. Roll the dough over the base, keeping the centre ⅛ in (0.25 cm) thick. Spread the pizza sauce evenly over the pizza dough but leave the edges clear. Place the onion on top, followed by the mushrooms, pepper and cheese, and the anchovies, tuna or chicken if used. Finally, sprinkle the remaining oregano on top. Bake the pizza in the preheated oven for 10 minutes or until the cheese is golden brown.

Spanish Vegetable Tortilla
Serves 4

A tortilla in Spain (in Mexico it is a cornmeal pancake) is really a thick omelette which can be eaten hot or cold. Cut into wedges and wrapped, tortillas make a convenient picnic food. The recipe given here is for a light, colourful tortilla, but it is still a recognizable cousin of those potato-thick tortillas, served in Spanish bars as *tapas*, which go so well with coarse red wine and strong bread.

5 eggs, beaten
3 egg yolks
2 tablespoons natural yoghurt
4 tablespoons fresh or skimmed milk
salt and freshly ground black pepper to taste
2 tablespoons olive oil
1 medium onion, peeled and thinly sliced
1 clove garlic, peeled and crushed
4 oz (100 g) new potatoes, cooked and thinly sliced
3 oz (75 g) cooked peas or defrosted frozen peas
1 small green pepper, seeded and finely chopped
1 small red pepper, seeded and finely chopped
2 oz (50 g) pimento-stuffed olives, halved
3 oz (75 g) lettuce, finely shredded
2 oz (50 g) Cheddar cheese, grated

Beat the eggs with the egg yolks, yoghurt, milk and salt and black pepper. Heat the oil in a large frying pan, preferably a non-stick one, then add the onion and garlic and fry gently for 3 minutes. Add the potatoes, peas, green and red peppers, olives and lettuce and stir-fry for 2–3 minutes. Pour the egg mixture into the pan and cook it until it is set on the underside. Sprinkle the tortilla with grated cheese and place it under a preheated grill until it is just set in the centre and golden brown on the top. The tortilla can be cut into wedges and eaten straight away or served cold.

Spinach and Mushroom Gougères
Serves 4

Surprisingly, choux pastry is one of the easier types of pastry to get absolutely right. It also gives the impression of great culinary skill. Once the technique is mastered, the horizons are wide open for sweet profiteroles, éclairs and so on.

PASTRY SHELLS
½ pint (275 ml) water
3 oz (75 g) butter, cut into pieces
1 teaspoon salt
2 turns of the pepper mill
grating of nutmeg
4 oz (100 g) sifted white flour
4 standard eggs
2 oz (50 g) Cheddar cheese
beaten egg for glazing

FILLING
4 spring onions
1 oz (25 g) butter
1 lb (450 g) fresh spinach leaves
6 oz (175 g) mushrooms
6 oz (175 g) low- or medium-fat cream cheese
milk
salt and fresh ground black pepper

PASTRY SHELLS

Preheat the oven to 220°C (425°F, gas mark 7). In a heavy-bottomed saucepan bring the water to the boil with the butter, salt, pepper and nutmeg. Remove the pan from the heat and pour the flour into the mixture. Mix vigorously and thoroughly, and then return the pan to a moderately high heat for about 2 minutes, until the mixture forms a solid mass and leaves the sides of the pan. Remove the pan from the heat and beat in one of the eggs, stirring until it is well absorbed. Repeat with the other three eggs and then continue beating for another minute until the mixture is really well blended. Finally, beat in the grated cheese.

Butter a large baking sheet. Put the mixture into a piping bag with a wide nozzle and pipe 12 circular mounds about 2 in (5 cm) in diameter (alternatively drop the mixture into neat piles with a spoon), keeping the mounds about 2 in (5 cm) apart. Gently glaze each mound with a little beaten egg. Any surplus pastry can be either frozen raw or cooked. Place the pastries in the preheated oven for about 20 minutes until they are well risen and golden brown. Remove them from the oven and pierce the side of each one with a sharp knife. Put them back in the oven with heat off and the door ajar for 10 minutes.

FILLING

Chop the white and some of the green parts of the spring onions and sweat them gently in the butter. Meanwhile, thoroughly wash and cook the spinach with no extra water in a covered saucepan. Drain it in a colander and press it to get rid of any excess water. Finely chop the mushrooms and add them to the spring onions, keeping the pan covered. Cook them for 5 minutes. On a wooden board finely chop the spinach and then, away from the heat, mix it with the mushrooms and spring onions. Add the cream cheese and mix well. Season with salt and black pepper.

To assemble, stuff the cooked gougère shells with the filling and gently reheat them before serving.

VARIATIONS

The fillings for this recipe are endless. Fish or minced chicken combined with a tasty, ricy sauce is ideal.

Sweet Potato and Walnut Soufflé

Serves 4

Sweet potatoes are now readily available in ethnic food stores. They give this soufflé an exotic flavour, and its sweetness is often enjoyed by children.

12 oz (350 g) sweet potatoes
1 oz (25 g) butter or vegetable margarine, melted
1 fl oz (25 ml) warm milk
2 tablespoons dried breadcrumbs
½ oz (12.5 g) flour
¼ pint (150 ml) milk
1½ oz (40 g) chopped walnuts
pinch nutmeg
salt and freshly ground black pepper to taste
3 large eggs, separated

Preheat the oven to 200°C (400°F, gas mark 6). Peel and boil the sweet potatoes until tender (about 20–25 minutes). Drain them and rub them through a sieve. Beat in half the butter and the warm milk to form a fairly soft purée. Prepare a 7 in (18 cm) soufflé dish by brushing it with melted butter and dusting it with breadcrumbs. Use the rest of the butter and the flour to make a roux and cook for 1 minute. Remove the roux from the heat, stir in the milk and bring the mixture to the boil, stirring continuously until it is smooth and thick. Add the sweet potato purée, walnuts, nutmeg and salt and black pepper. Allow the mixture to cool slightly and then beat in the egg yolks. Whisk the egg whites until they are stiff but not dry and fold them into the sweet potato mixture. Pour the mixture into the prepared soufflé dish and place it in the middle of the preheated oven. Cook for 20–25 minutes or until the soufflé is well risen and golden brown.

Lettuce Soufflé
Serves 4

A low-fat, elegant dish, just right for a healthy dinner party.

8 oz (225 g) iceberg lettuce, chopped
2 oz (50 g) butter or vegetable margarine
¾ oz (20 g) flour
salt and freshly ground black pepper to taste
¼ pint (150 ml) semi-skimmed milk
1 teaspoon Worcestershire sauce
4 oz (100 g) Cheddar cheese, grated
4 eggs, separated
2 oz (50 g) Parmesan cheese, grated
¾ teaspoon cream of tartar

Preheat the oven to 190°C (375°F, gas mark 5). Cook the chopped lettuce in very little water until just tender, then drain. Add ½ oz (12.5 g) butter or margarine, cook and stir until any water has disappeared. In a separate pan melt the remaining butter or margarine and blend in the flour, salt and black pepper. Cook over a low heat for 3–5 minutes. Blend in the milk and Worcestershire sauce. Cook, stirring, until the sauce has thickened. Remove the pan from the heat. Add the cheese and stir until it has melted. Beat in the egg yolks one at a time, then add the cooked lettuce. Butter a 7 in (18 cm) soufflé dish or mould, then coat the sides with half the Parmesan. Beat the egg whites until they are foamy, add the cream of tartar and a pinch of salt, and whip the whites until they are stiff. Stir a quarter of the whipped whites into the lettuce mixture, then fold in the remainder. Pour the mixture into the prepared soufflé dish or mould, smooth the top and sprinkle it with the remaining Parmesan. Bake the soufflé in the middle of the preheated oven for 30–40 minutes until well risen and golden brown.

FISH AND SHELLFISH

Fish are a good source of protein, vitamins and minerals and the fat that they contain is high in polyunsaturates and thus unlikely to contribute to fat-related disease. Fish are also quick to prepare and cook, an extremely versatile food and, of equal importance, a joy to eat.

Cod, haddock and plaice are by far the most frequently eaten fish, and are those that consumers, quite naturally, think of first when cooking at home. In restaurants, on the other hand, a much wider range is offered, and there is every reason to encourage cooks at home to be more imaginative in their choice of species.

Fish are classified into three main groups: white fish, in which the oil is found in the liver; oily fish, in which the oil is dispersed throughout the flesh, and shellfish. The fat content of white fish is normally less than 5 per cent and sometimes as low as 1 per cent. Oily fish contain less fat than many cuts of meat and of the 20 per cent fat content of, say, herring, only a fifth is saturated.

Your fishmonger will stock a wide selection of each of the three groups of fish and a selection of smoked fish. Availability and price depend on the season, the weather and the region of the country you live in. Ask your fishmonger's advice on selecting and preparing fish and take advantage of the lower price of some species. For instance, instead of cod and haddock you could try coley, pollack or ling. Remember also that, as long as they belong to the same general group, different species of fish are interchangeable in recipes. In many of the recipes given here a number of species are suggested.

White fish are divided into two types of species: round and flat. The large round species, such as coley and cod, are usually sold in steaks, cutlets or fillets, which can be skinned if desired. The small round species, such as whiting and haddock, are sold in fillets and, again, can be skinned. The fishmonger will also clean and trim the whole fish for you, removing head, fins and tail ready for cooking.

The larger flat-fish varieties, such as halibut and turbot, are usually sold in fillets and steaks, and are trimmed as required. The small flat fish, such as plaice and lemon sole, are usually sold whole and trimmed or filleted as required. Dover sole is usually sold whole. These species are ideal for stuffing.

The oily fish species, such as herring and mackerel, are important sources of vitamins A and D.

There is a wide range of shellfish species, which are often sold prepared and sometimes cooked (e.g. crabs and prawns) ready for use. You can ask your fishmonger to clean or dress any shellfish for you. Shellfish are versatile and can be served in a variety of ways; often only a very small quantity is sufficient to create an impressive dish.

A small variety of fish is sold preserved or cured by salting or marinating, such as herrings, or by smoking, such as cod, haddock, whiting and kippers. There are two methods of smoking – cold and hot. Cold-smoked fish, such as kippers and kippered mackerel, have a smoky flavour, but are still raw and must be cooked. Hot-smoked fish, such as mackerel, are smoked at higher temperatures so the flesh cooks in the heat and is ready to eat.

COMMON WHITE FISH

Round: sea bass, sea bream, cod, coley, conger eel, haddock, hake, huss, ling, monkfish, grey mullet, red mullet, pollack, skate, whiting.

Flat: brill, dab, flounder, halibut, megrim, plaice, lemon or Dover sole, turbot, witch.

COMMON OILY FISH

Herring, mackerel, sardine, sprat, tuna.

COMMON SHELLFISH

Cockles, crab, lobster, mussels, oysters, prawns, scallops, scampi (Dublin Bay prawns), shrimps.

TO CLEAN FISH

Either ask your fishmonger to do it or follow these instructions: For round, white and oily fish, remove any scales by scraping from tail to head with the dull edge of a knife. Flat fish are not normally scaled. Rinse the fish frequently while doing this to wash off the loosened scales. To remove the innards from a round fish, cut along the abdomen from a point beneath the gills to half-way to the tail. Scoop out the innards with your fingers or a table knife and rinse the cavity under running water. Cut off the head and tail if desired. Cut off the fins and gills. For the same operation with a flat fish, cut open the entrail cavity which lies beneath the gills near the head. Remove the entrails as above. Cut off the head and tail if desired. Cut off the gills and fins.

TO FILLET A ROUND FISH

Clean the fish as above. Cut off the head and tail or make a semicircular cut around the head on both sides. With the tail facing towards you cut down the length of the backbone, keeping the knife on top of the backbone with the blade pressing flat on it. Lift the fillet off and cut it clear from the rib bones using the point of the knife in a stroking action. Turn the fish over and remove the other fillet in the same way. Run your fingers over both fillets to locate any remaining bones and pull them out with your fingers or a pair of tweezers.

TO QUARTER-CUT FILLET A FLAT FISH

Clean the fish as above. The head and tail may be left on. Using a sharp, thin knife, cut around the head, then cut down the length of the back of the fish following and just reaching the line of the backbone. Turn the knife flat and insert it under the flesh on the left-hand side of the fish at the head end, so that the blade is just pressing on the bones. Cut the flesh clear in one piece with two or three strokes of the knife. Repeat for the right-hand fillet. Now turn the fish over and repeat the operation for the other side of the fish so that you end up with four fillets.

COOKING METHODS

A number of basic cooking methods are suitable for virtually all types of fish, whether whole, filleted, cutlets or steaks. However, there is one golden rule when cooking fish – never overcook. As fish are naturally tender, they should be cooked for as short a time as possible because prolonged cooking not only toughens the flesh, but also impairs the flavour, texture and nutritional value. Remember, when cooking with fish, one species of the same type can usually be substituted for another.

DEEP-FRYING

Deep-frying is a traditional and popular method of cooking fish best suited to fillets. The fish must be coated prior to cooking to prevent the flesh breaking up and also provide a flavoursome crust. Suitable coatings are breadcrumbs or batter.

1 Preheat the oil to between 172–190°C (360–375°F), depending on the size of the fish.
2 Coat the fish in egg and breadcrumbs or in batter.
3 Check the temperature of the fat before frying. If the fat is not hot enough, the batter will be heavy and soggy; if too hot, the coating will brown too quickly before the fish is cooked.
4 Fry for 4–5 minutes depending on the thickness of the fillets.

SHALLOW-FRYING

A quick method best used for fillets and steaks. As with deep-frying, the fish should first be coated to protect the flesh and seal in the flavour.

1 Coat the prepared fish either with a dusting of seasoned flour or with egg and breadcrumbs.
2 Shallow-fry in preheated oil for 5–10 minutes depending on the thickness of the fillet. For larger, thicker fillets or whole fish, start over a high heat to allow the coating to set, then reduce the heat and cook until the flesh is tender.
3 Drain well before serving.

BRAISING

Braising is an all-in-one-pan cooking method in which any variety of fish, together with a small selection of vegetables, is cooked in a casserole on the hob or in the oven.

1 If using the oven, preheat it to 190°C (375°F, gas mark 5).
2 Heat a little butter in a saucepan and lightly brown the chopped vegetables.
3 Cut the fish into large chunks or steaks and add them to the pan, together with seasonings and liquids in the form of stock or wine. (If using the oven, transfer the browned vegetables to an ovenproof casserole, together with the prepared fish, seasoning and liquids).

4 Place the lid on the saucepan or casserole and cook until fish and vegetables are tender.

MICROWAVING

Fish cooks well in a microwave oven, retaining its flavour and juices. Microwaves are particularly useful for baking, braising and poaching fish.

POACHING

One of the gentlest methods of cooking fish, poaching is ideal for larger whole fish or fish fillets such as smoked haddock. Suitable liquids for poaching are fish stock, water, milk or wine, together with seasoning.

1 Warm the liquid in a saucepan.
2 Place the prepared fish in the pan and, if poaching fillets, top them with a knob of butter. Large whole fish should be poached in a fish kettle.
3 Poach for 5 – 8 minutes depending on the thickness of the fillet. Never let the liquid boil as this results in the flesh flaking and a dry texture.
4 Drain off any liquid that remains after cooking and use it to make an accompanying sauce.

BAKING

Fish that is cooked in the oven is said to be baked rather than roasted. This method is suitable for whole fish, fillets and steaks.

1 For large whole fish, preheat the oven to 180°C (350°F, gas mark 4). For smaller fish or fillets, preheat to 200°C (400°F, gas mark 6).
2 Season the prepared fish well and place them in an ovenproof casserole with a knob of butter.
3 Pour a little stock or wine, or a mixture of both, over the fish to baste them. If using flat fish fillets, a stuffing enhances the flavour and also helps to retain moisture.
4 Bake the fish in the oven for 15 – 20 minutes. Any remaining juices should be used to flavour an accompanying sauce.

GRILLING

A very quick method of cooking fillets, cutlets or whole fish by the radiant heat of a hot grill.

1 Line the grill pan with foil and brush the grill rack with oil to prevent the fish sticking. Preheat the grill.
2 Season the prepared fish. If grilling whole fish, make two or three slashes along their backs to allow the heat to penetrate.
3 Brush the fish with melted butter or a marinade to help retain moisture.
4 Cook under a moderate to hot grill, turning the fish once, for 8 – 10 minutes.

STEAMING

Steaming is an ideal method for fillets which are either rolled or folded, and then placed in the steamer.

1 Heat the water in the base of the steamer to simmering point.
2 Season the prepared fish well, then place them in the steamer and put on the tightly fitting lid.
3 Steam for 10–15 minutes, remembering to keep the water topped up.
4 If you do not possess a steamer, you can steam the fish between two plates over a saucepan of simmering water.

Smoked Fish

In the days before refrigeration fish had to be cured to keep them in good condition for their journey from the port to inland market. Nowadays smoking is used mainly to give fish a characteristic, pleasant flavour. The preservation effect is only slight and smoked fish products keep in good condition for a little longer than the fresh fish from which they are made.

THE SMOKING PROCESS

There are two methods of smoking fish in the UK:
Cold smoking, in which the fish are cured by smoking at an air temperature not higher than 33°C to avoid cooking the flesh. It is recommended that cold-smoked products, with the exception of the smoked salmon, be cooked before they are eaten.
Hot smoking, in which the fish are smoked at a temperature of 70–80°C at some stage during the process in order to cook the flesh. Hot-smoked products do not require further cooking and are ideal for salads and pâtes.

When smoking, prepared fish are first of all brined, which gives the finished fish their attractive gloss. This involves soaking the fish in a strong brine which sometimes contains a dye to supplement the natural colouring process. The length of time that fish are immersed in the brine depends on the size and thickness of the individual fillet or fish.

The fish are then drained, hung on racks in a kiln and exposed to smoke from burning wood or peat for 5–6 hours.

CHOOSING SMOKED FISH

The surface should be bright, glossy and clean. The flesh should be firm and springy to the touch. Good-quality smoked fish should have a pleasant, smoky smell.

As well as the popular smoked haddock, kippers and smoked mackerel, there are a number of other products available:

Finnan haddock is named after the village of Findon, south of Aberdeen. The headless split haddock are first of all lightly brined and then cold-smoked until straw-coloured. They are not usually dyed. Finnan haddock is also known as Findon haddock, or Finnan haddie.

Smokies are cleaned and headed haddock which are tied together in pairs by the tail, brined and hot-smoked.

Bloaters are whole ungutted herring which are lightly salted and smoked. Because the gut is not removed, the fish have a gamey flavour.

Red herrings are whole ungutted herrings which are heavily brined until they turn red and then cold-smoked in a traditional kiln for 2–3 weeks until quite firm. They are also called hard-smoked herrings.

Buckling are headless herring which are hot-smoked and therefore ready for eating.

Smoked sprats are whole sprats brined and lightly smoked so that they keep their silvery appearance.

Shellfish

Buy shellfish live or freshly cooked. Cook them simply and eat them as soon as possible after purchase.

CRAB

Three kinds of edible crab are found around the coast of Britain: the velvet crab, the spider crab and the brown crab. The first two are prized on the Continent and are accordingly difficult to find in the shops; the last is abundant round the entire seaboard and is sold alive, boiled or dressed.

Cock (male) crabs are larger than hens (females) and have bigger claws; during the summer months the hen's shell is lined with delicious pink coral. Judge crabs not by their size but by their weight – a good crab should be heavy for its size – and there should be no sound of water inside when you shake the shell. Make sure the shell is not cracked or holed, or the meat will be soft and watery. Ensure that the crab has all its claws.

There are two types of meat in a crab: white (found in the legs and claws) and brown (the body meat). The brown is stronger in flavour than the white and has a creamier texture; when a crab is dressed the white meat is usually arranged decoratively with the brown.

LOBSTERS AND LANGOUSTINE

It takes around seven years for a lobster to reach marketable size. Although lobsters have been bred in captivity, they are not yet farmed in the full commercial sense, so any you see in the shops are wild creatures.

Most of the British catch goes to the Continent, where the massive demand increases both their price and their rarity at home. Abroad they are sold live, whereas here they mostly come freshly boiled; during cooking their colour changes from deep blue to scarlet.

Also known as Norway lobsters, Dublin Bay prawns, or scampi, langoustines are arguably the most handsome of the crustaceans. They are like small lobsters with elongated claws and they retain their splendid peach and coral colours after cooking. This makes them an attractive addition to any mixed fish dish. They commonly appear peeled, as well, as breaded (tails only) scampi.

Langoustines are trawled for and caught in special pots. Squat lobsters, a little-known British crustacean, creep into the same pots. They are particularly sought after for Nouvelle Cuisine. Availability is likely to be limited.

There is not enough meat in either the head or the claws of these smaller crustaceans to warrant the effort of picking it out, although it is perfectly edible.

MUSSELS

Mussels cling to the sea bed or hang from rocks or ropes. Their shells range in colour from blue-black to golden tortoiseshell. They take about two years to reach maturity, and have an excellent, slightly sweet flavour.

Their shells should be undamaged when you buy them and must be tightly closed or should close when tapped. Any that remain closed after you have cooked them must be discarded.

Some cooks leave them overnight in a bucket of water to remove any grit, but since most mussels sold in the shops will have been purified, this is usually unnecessary. After scrubbing the shells rigorously, you must pull out as much as you can of the wiry beard which sprouts from the mussel's straight edge.

Mussels produce a surprising quantity of moisture as they cook, so you only need a small amount of liquid to poach or steam them. They should be cooked in a heavy pan over a high heat for just as long as it takes for their shells to open – a matter of minutes. Overcooked mussels tend to be rubbery, so beware of this risk.

SCALLOPS AND OYSTERS

Two kinds of scallops are caught around our coast (the smaller, rounder, pink shells are called queen scallops), and two kinds of oyster are sold, the native and the Pacific. Princess scallops, one of the latest developments, are also now becoming available.

Scallops can be bought either in their shells or ready prepared. If the former, they can be opened by placing them, convex shell down, in a warm oven. After a few moments the shells will open wide enough for a sharp knife to be inserted and the fish's firm white muscle cut as close to the shell as possible. Any liquor that has collected in the shell should be kept.

To clean them, cut away the grey-brown frill and black intestinal thread which runs from the central white muscle to the base of the coral tongue.

Scallops may be poached, sautéed or baked, but it is important not to overcook them – an overcooked scallop loses flavour and has a rubbery texture.

Gourmets believe that oysters are best eaten raw. The shells should be opened immediately before they are served, and you would do well to ask your fishmonger to demonstrate how to do this, for it requires a certain knack. They are served on their own cupped shells, on a bed of crushed ice, with chunks of lemon, slices of brown bread and butter and a dash of cayenne pepper or Tabasco sauce.

Oysters have the flavour of the sea and when they are cooked this becomes even stronger. Just three or four oysters can enliven the flavour of a large steak and kidney pie.

CLAMS

These are caught mainly in the Solent and off the north-west coast of Scotland. Small clams are eaten raw and large ones cooked. They are available fresh all the year round, but you may have to ask your fishmonger to obtain them specially.

SHRIMPS AND PRAWNS

Shrimps inhabiting rock pools around the entire coast of Britain are the joy of children on holiday with shrimping nets. Nowadays they are fished commercially from the shallow waters of the Wash or Morecambe Bay.

They are our smallest crustaceans, pink or brown when cooked. Try to buy them fresh-cooked, whether peeled or whole (remember you eat only the tail).

This is also true of their larger relative, the prawn, most of which are caught of the north and west coasts of Scotland and sold quick-frozen, either peeled or whole.

The most popular hors d'oeuvre in Britain is prawn or shrimp cocktail, though, sadly, the sauce they are served in is usually too strong to permit the flavour of the main ingredients to be savoured. Good-quality mayonnaise and a little cream make all the difference.

SQUID

There are several varieties of squid caught round the British coast at different times of the year. They are in fact molluscs, but with an internal shell which has been reduced to a clear tube called a pen. This is removed before cooking. Because of the inconsistency of landings, they may not always be available fresh, so make the most of them when you see them as they are excellent eating.

WINKLES, WHELKS AND COCKLES

Winkles are gathered from rock pools on lonely strands; whelks live off shore and are caught in special pots; cockles are fished commercially around the Wash and the Thames estuary and off the shores of South Wales.

All three make an attractive and unusual addition to fish dishes such as paella or bouillabaisse (fish soup), but all three may be eaten on their own.

Like so many of our shellfish, winkles and whelks are highly sought after on the Continent. Both should be steamed for a few moments, extracted from their shells with a pin or small fork and then sprinkled with lemon juice, butter and black pepper. Whelks are very much larger than winkles and are sometimes sliced before serving.

It is difficult to find fresh cockles these days – they are usually sold bottled in brine or vinegar. The former is better, as vinegar tends to mask their delicate flavour. Sometimes you can buy them frozen – in which case try them heated and tossed in a little garlic butter.

Indian Spiced Hake
Serves 4

Serve with rice and other traditional curry accompaniments such as chutney, chapattis and cucumber in yoghurt.

1 tablespoon sunflower oil
1/2 large onion, sliced
1/2 oz (15 g) medium-hot curry powder
1/2 oz (15 g) flour
1 tablespoon tomato purée
1/4 pint (150 ml) fish stock
7 oz (200 g) tin tomatoes
1 dessert apple, cored and diced
1 1/2 oz (40 g) raisins
salt and freshly ground black pepper to taste
4 × 6 – 8 oz (175 – 225 g) hake steaks

Heat the oil in a large shallow pan and fry the onion until transparent. Stir in the curry powder, flour and tomato purée and cook for 1–2 minutes. Gradually add the stock and tomatoes. Bring the sauce to the boil, then add the apple, raisins and seasoning. Reduce the heat and simmer for 10 minutes until the sauce thickens slightly. Add the fish to the sauce and simmer for 8 – 10 minutes or until cooked.

Poached Hake with Orange and Dill Sauce
Serves 4

Hake is a large seawater fish of the cod family and it can be used just as well in cod or haddock recipes. It has good white flesh and is an excellent fish for frying, grilling or casseroling, although poaching is the most popular.

4 × 6–8 oz (175–225 g) hake steaks
½ pint (300 ml) fish or chicken stock
2 tablespoons fresh dill
salt and freshly ground black pepper to taste
1 tablespoon cornflour
3 fl oz (70 ml) fresh orange juice
2 oranges, peeled and cut into segments

Poach the hake steaks in the fish stock with half the dill and salt and black pepper for 8–10 minutes. Drain, reserving the poaching liquid, and then transfer the hake to a warmed serving dish. Mix the cornflour to a paste with the orange juice and add it to the poaching liquid with the orange segments. Cook, stirring, until the sauce is thickened and hot. Spoon some of the sauce over the fish and garnish with the remaining fresh dill. Serve the rest of the sauce separately.

BARBECUED FISH

Barbecued fish are one of the treats of summer. Oily fish such as herring and mackerel are particularly well suited to this method of cooking because the oils they contain help to keep the flesh moist during cooking. Here are a few useful tips to remember when barbecuing fish; they are followed by two recipes.

1 Either wrap whole fish in foil or use a fish clamp which allows the fish to be turned, if necessary, during cooking.
2 Remember to season the fish before enclosing it in the foil or the clamp. The fish can also be marinated before cooking, perhaps in a mixture of wine, fish stock, herbs and a little oil. When using a clamp the fish can be basted during cooking.
3 Remember to score the fish at its thickest part to ensure even cooking.
4 Fillets can be wrapped in foil with herbs and seasonings and then cooked on top of the barbecue. Alternatively, the fillets can be cut into chunks and threaded onto kebab sticks with a selection of vegetables and then cooked over the barbecue. Always start and finish the kebab with something solid such as onion quarters as this helps to keep the rest of the ingredients secure on the skewer.
5 Lastly, remember that the heat from a barbecue can be quite fierce, so take care not to overcook the fish.

Easy Barbecued Fish

Small grey mullet, herring or mackerel, scaled and cleaned (12 oz–1 lb fish per person)
sprigs of fresh herbs

MARINADE/BASTE
grated rind and juice of 1 lemon
3 tablespoons sunflower oil
fresh mixed herbs, chopped
salt and freshly ground black pepper to taste

Remove the head from the fish, if preferred. Mix together the marinade/baste ingredients. Cut three slits on each side of the fish and, if time permits, lay the fish in a shallow dish and cover it with the marinade. Chill for approximately 1 hour. Cook for 10–15 minutes under a moderate grill or over a charcoal fire, basting with the marinade and turning once.

Barbecued or Gilled Fish Kebabs with Marinade

Serves 2–4

4 × 8 oz (225 g) herring or mackerel, cleaned and filleted
3 small onions, quartered
4 tomatoes, halved
salt and freshly ground black pepper to taste

MARINADE
½ pint (300 ml) fish or chicken stock
6 tablespoons tomato ketchup
2 tablespoons wine vinegar
2 tablespoons Worcestershire sauce
2 tablespoons brown sugar
2 drops Tabasco (optional)
2 tablespoons tomato purée
1 tablespoon cornflour

Cut the herring or mackerel crosswise into four pieces. To make the marinade, mix together all the ingredients except the cornflour and marinate the mackerel or herring in them for about 1 hour. Drain the fish, reserving the marinade, and thread the pieces on skewers, alternating them with the onion and tomatoes. Grill or barbecue for 10 minutes, basting with the sauce and turning the skewers. Transfer the kebabs to a serving dish. Blend the cornflour with a little water and mix to a smooth paste. Add this to the remaining marinade with any juices from the grill pan. Heat, stirring, until the sauce has thickened. Serve the kebabs with the marinade sauce.

Herring Brochettes
Serves 2–4

This recipe is suitable for use with a domestic grill or a barbecue. Serve the brochettes with rice and a salad.

4 herring, cleaned and boned
1 large red onion
2 lemons
8 bay leaves
1 tablespoon sunflower oil
1 tablespoon lemon juice
salt and freshly ground black pepper to taste
pinch of cayenne pepper

Cut the herring crosswise into four pieces. Cut the onion into eighths and the lemons into wedges. Thread the herring, onion, lemons and bay leaves alternately onto skewers. Mix together the sunflower oil, lemon juice and seasoning. Use this dressing to baste the brochettes while grilling or barbecuing for about 10 minutes. Turn the brochettes three or four times during cooking.

Kedgeree
Serves 4

Kedgeree is a traditional English breakfast dish which was developed from the Indian rice dish *kichiri* (see p. 76) by our colonial forebears. Here is a recipe for a modern low-fat version that can be served at any time of the day.

6 oz (175 g) long-grain brown or white rice
4 tablespoons sunflower oil
1¼ lb (700 g) smoked haddock, skinned and shredded
2 hardboiled eggs, chopped
2 teaspoons lemon juice
1 tablespoon chopped parsley
salt and freshly ground black pepper to taste
lemon or lime slices to garnish

Cook the rice in boiling water until tender. Drain and set aside. Heat the oil in a large saucepan and gently sauté the fish for 5 minutes. Add the cooked rice, eggs, lemon juce and parsley, and stir. Season with salt and black pepper and serve immediately garnished with lemon or lime slices.

Note: Butter may be substituted for sunflower oil for a more authentic flavour.

Fish and Pasta
Serves 4

Make this simple but tasty dish with coley or, for a more expensive treat, monkfish. Macaroni and fish are cooked together in a garlic-flavoured tomato sauce.

1 oz (25 g) butter or vegetable oil
1–2 cloves garlic, crushed
2–3 sticks celery, chopped
14 oz (380 g) tin tomatoes
1/2 pint (275 ml) fish or chicken stock
4 oz (100 g) macaroni (white or wholewheat)
1 bay leaf
7 oz (200 g) tin sweetcorn, drained
1 1/2 lb (675 g) coley fillets or monkfish, skinned, and cubed
salt and freshly ground black pepper to taste
finely chopped fresh coriander or parsley to garnish

Heat the butter or oil in a large saucepan and sauté the garlic and celery until softened. Add the tomatoes, stock, macaroni and bay leaf. Cover and simmer for 5 minutes for plain macaroni and 8 minutes for wholewheat macaroni. Add the sweetcorn and fish, stir gently, cover and simmer for a further 5 minutes or until the fish and pasta are tender. Serve immediately, garnished with parsley or coriander.

Spiced Marinated Plaice
Serves 4

Thin strips of filleted plaice are marinated in a chilli, lemon and olive oil dressing and then served with a green salad. Serve with crusty wholemeal bread as a light meal or starter. This is a delicious and unusual way to serve plaice.

12 oz (375 g) plaice fillet, skinned
2 tablespoons soya sauce
3 tablespoons olive oil
2 teaspoons wholegrain mustard
1 large clove garlic, crushed
2 red chillies, finely chopped
4 tablespoons lemon juice
small piece fresh ginger root, crushed
salt and freshly ground black pepper to taste
6 oz (175 g) lettuce, finely shredded
3 spring onions, cut diagonally
3 oz (75 g) button mushrooms, thinly sliced
fresh coriander to garnish

Cut the plaice fillet into long thin strips and place them in a shallow dish. Mix the soya sauce with the olive oil, mustard, garlic, chillies, lemon juice, ginger, salt and black pepper. Spoon the marinade over the strips of plaice. Cover them with cling film and chill for 4 hours or overnight (the fish will turn opaque). Mix the shredded lettuce with the spring onions and sliced mushrooms and arrange these as a border around the edge of four medium-sized plates. Drain the marinated fish strips of their juices and place some in the centre of each plate. Trickle some of the spiced marinade over the fish and the lettuce and garnish with the coriander.

TRADITIONAL FISH AND CHIPS

A recipe for perfect chips follows, together with one for deep-frying fish in batter, the only real partner to a plate of chips. Note the fish batter contains a small amount of light ale – this gives it extra flavour and a lighter texture.

Chipped Potatoes
Serves 2 – 4

1 lb (450 g) potatoes (Marais Piper or Desirées are the best)
oil

Cut the potatoes into ½ in (1 cm) fingers and place them in a bowl of iced water for about 10 minutes. Drain and dry them on a clean teatowel. Place the oil in a deep pan – 1 ½ pints (900 ml) for ½ lb (225 g) chips in an 8 in (20 cm) standard chip pan and heat to 190°C (375°F). Add the chips and deep fry until fat stops bubbling furiously. Remove the basket and allow the fat to reheat to 190°C (375°F) then cook the chips for a further 5 minutes until crisp and golden brown. Drain and serve.

Fish in Beer Batter
Serves 4

4 × 6 oz (175 g) white fish fillets, (plaice, cod, haddock or huss)
oil for deep-frying
seasoned flour

BEER BATTER
4 oz (100 g) plain flour
pinch salt
2 tablespoons oil
¼ pint (150 ml) light ale
1 large egg white

Preheat the oil for deep-fat frying to 190°C (375°F). To prepare the batter, sieve the flour and salt into a bowl. Make a well in the centre, pour the oil and beer into the well, and carefully mix them into the flour. Whisk the egg white until stiff and fold it into the batter. Coat the fish fillets in seasoned flour then dip them into the batter, drain and lower them into the hot oil, cooking one or two fish fillets at a time. Fry until the batter is crisp and golden. Remove the fish from the oil and drain on absorbent paper.

Herring Stuffed with Cream Cheese and Coconut
Serves 4

An interesting combination of ingredients to make a delicious and nutritious dish. Serve with a green salad and crunchy bread.

5 oz (150 g) low-fat cream cheese
½ small red pepper, seeded and diced
½ small green pepper, seeded and diced
1 tablespoon desiccated coconut
pinch oregano
salt and freshly ground black pepper to taste
4 herring, cleaned
coconut for sprinkling

Preheat the oven to 190°C (375°F, gas mark 5). Place the cheese in a bowl and mix in the peppers and coconut. Season the mixture with a pinch of oregano and salt and black pepper. Remove the heads from the fish if desired. Fill the inside of the herring with the cream cheese mixture and place them in an ovenproof dish. Sprinkle each fish with coconut and bake uncovered for 25–30 minutes until the fish is cooked and the coconut is golden brown.

Chilled Herring and Yoghurt
Serves 4

Herring are poached in tarragon-flavoured wine stock, chilled and then served with a yoghurt and cooking liquor sauce. Serve as a salad or a light dish for a summer evening.

4 × 8 oz (225 g) herring, boned and cut into strips
1 medium-sized onion, thinly sliced
1 teaspoon tarragon
6 peppercorns
salt to taste
¼ pint (150 ml) fish or chicken stock
¼ pint (150 ml) wine vinegar
¼ pint (150 ml) natural yoghurt
3 oz (75 g) seedless green grapes

Preheat the oven to 160°C (325°F, gas mark 3). Place the fish, onion slices, seasonings and liquids in an ovenproof dish. Cover, and poach in the oven for 30 minutes. Remove from the oven and chill. When chilled, drain the fish, reserving the liquid, and arrange them on a serving dish. Strain the liquid and blend 2 tablespoons of the strained liquid with the yoghurt. Pour the sauce over the fish and serve garnished with grapes.

Red Mullet and Goats' Cheese in Lettuce Leaves

Serves 6

Red mullet is no relation to the larger grey mullet. It is a smallish fish weighing 1–2 lb (450–900 g) with tasty firm white flesh. It is normally cooked whole.

6 medium-sized red mullet, scaled, gutted and cleaned
salt and freshly ground black pepper to taste
2 oz (50 g) chèvre cheese, crumbled
grated rind of ½ lemon
1 teaspoon Pesto sauce (a basil, pine-nut and garlic sauce,
more commonly served with pasta) (optional)
4 oz (100 g) iceberg lettuce, finely chopped
12 large green lettuce leaves
⅓ pint (200 ml) dry white wine

Preheat the oven to 180°C (350°F, gas mark 4). Season the mullet inside and out. Mix the chèvre cheese with the lemon rind, Pesto if used, the finely chopped iceberg lettuce and salt and black pepper. Fill the cavity of each red mullet with the cheese stuffing. Blanch the lettuce leaves in boiling water for 1 minute and refresh immediately in cold water. Drain thoroughly. Wrap each stuffed red mullet in two lettuce leaves and lay them side by side in an ovenproof dish. Spoon the white wine over the fish and cover the dish with foil. Cook for 30–35 minutes until the mullet are just tender. Lift the mullet onto a serving dish and serve with the cooking juices.

Jamaican Braised Mackerel

Serves 2

This is a chilli-hot fish dish. Serve it with cucumber in yoghurt, which helps to cool the mouth. If you prefer mild food, reduce the amount of chilli pepper in the recipe.

2 × 12 oz (350 g) whole mackerel or grey mullet, cleaned and heads removed
salt and freshly ground black pepper to taste
4 spring onions, finely chopped
1–2 red or green chillies, finely chopped
1 clove garlic, crushed
pinch oregano
2 teaspoons lemon juice
1 oz (25 g) butter or polyunsaturated margarine
1 small onion, finely chopped
14 oz (400 g) tin chopped tomatoes
½–1 tablespoon chilli sauce

Make three diagonal cuts on one side of each fish. Season the fish inside and out with salt and black pepper. Combine the spring onions, chillies, garlic, oregano and lemon juice and press the mixture into the slits in the fish. Set aside in the refrigerator to marinate for 1 hour. Melt the butter or margarine in a large pan and fry the onion until soft. Add the tomatoes, chilli sauce and season with salt and black pepper. Lay the fish on top of the tomato sauce, cover and cook gently for 20 minutes or until the fish is tender. Serve immediately with the sauce from the pan.

Traditional Mackerel and Rhubarb Bake
Serves 2

1 lb (450 g) fresh rhubarb, topped and washed
1 oz (25 g) butter
1 medium onion, diced
8 oz (225 g) cooked long-grain rice
½ teaspoon rosemary
salt and freshly ground black pepper to taste
2 medium-sized or 4 small mackerel, boned
¼ pint (150 ml) water
½ oz (12.5 g) cornflour

Preheat the oven to 190°C (375°F, gas mark 5). Finely dice two sticks of rhubarb and chop the remainder into conventional pieces. Melt the butter in a pan and fry the onion and diced rhubarb for 2 minutes. Stir in the rice, rosemary and seasoning. Cover a baking sheet with oiled foil, lay the mackerel on top and stuff them with the rice mixture. Completely enclose the fish in foil, and bake for 30 minutes. Meanwhile, cook the remaining rhubarb in the water until soft. Mix the cornflour with a little water and blend it into the rhubarb. Bring to the boil stirring continuously. Serve with the cooked fish.

Skate with Courgette and Capers
Serves 4

Only the wings of skate are eaten. They have a sweetish flavour and the flesh easily falls away from the bones. In this simple but very flavoursome recipe the skate is baked and then served with a courgette, anchovy and caper sauce.

2 lb (900 g) skate wings (4 pieces), skinned
juice of 1 lemon
freshly ground black pepper to taste
2 oz (50 g) butter
1 medium onion, halved and thinly sliced
4 medium courgettes, cut into matchstick pieces
1 small tin achovies, chopped
1 tablespoon capers
lemon slices to garnish

Preheat the oven to 200°C (400°F, gas mark 6). Cover a baking tray with oiled foil. Wash the pieces of skate, lay them on the foil and sprinkle them with lemon juice and black pepper. Cover them with another piece of foil to make a parcel. Bake in the preheated oven for 15 minutes. Meanwhile melt the butter in a frying pan and fry the onion until it is transparent. Add the courgettes and cook gently for 2–3 minutes. Stir in the chopped anchovies and capers and season with more black pepper. Arrange the pieces of fish on a hot serving dish. Pour the juices from the fish into the courgette mixture and reheat quickly. When piping hot, spoon the dressing over the skate. Garnish with slices of lemon.

Note: As an alternative to skate wings, try cod steaks or cutlets. A cucumber cut into matchsticks may be used if courgettes are unavailable.

Skate wings are also delicious cold. Cook the fish, flake the flesh and mix with tomatoes, celery and cucumber for a delicious salad.

Fish Tikka
Serves 4

A simple but delicious Indian recipe for a dry curried cod steak. Serve with salad and yoghurt.

4 × 8 oz (225 g) cod steaks
1/4 pint (150 ml) natural yoghurt
1 clove garlic, crushed
1/2 teaspoon ground chilli
1 teaspoon garam masala
1/2 teaspoon ground ginger
1 tablespoon lemon juice
salt and freshly ground black pepper to taste
2–3 drops red food colouring (optional)

Place the fish in a shallow dish. In a small bowl mix together the remaining ingredients and pour them over the cod steaks. Cover and refrigerate for 2–4 hours. Place the steaks on a grill pan and grill them under a very low heat for 15–20 minutes. Turn the steaks three or four times during grilling.

Fish in Sweet and Spicy Sauce
Serves 4

This Southeast Asian recipe is honey sweet and spicy hot. Reduce the amount of chilli if you prefer mild food. The recipe is very versatile and you may use fillets of white fish such as cod, haddock, whiting, plaice or sole, or whole oily fish such as herring or mackerel.

2 lb (1 kg) fish fillets or 4 × 8 oz (225 g) small whole fish
salt
juice of 1 lemon
oil for shallow-frying

SAUCE
2 tablespoons oil
1 medium onion, finely sliced
2 cloves garlic, crushed
½–1 fresh or dried red chilli, seeded and finely chopped
8 oz (225 g) ripe tomatoes, peeled and chopped
½ teaspoon ground turmeric
¼ teaspoon ground ginger
1 tablespoon honey
2 tablespoons white vinegar
8 fl oz (225 ml) water
salt

If using whole fish, clean them first and then score the skin two or three times with a very sharp knife. Season the fish with salt, sprinkle them with lemon juice and set them aside. To make the sauce, heat the oil in a saucepan and sauté the onion, garlic and chilli for 2–3 minutes. Add the tomatoes, turmeric, ginger, honey and vinegar and cook, stirring, for 1–2 minutes. Add the water and salt and simmer the sauce for 15 minutes. Meanwhile heat the oil and shallow-fry the fillets or whole fish on both sides until they are browned and tender. Put the fish on a serving dish, cover them with the sauce and serve.

Grilled Mackerel with Hot Sauce
Serves 4

In this typical Southeast Asian method of grilling fish the mackerel is first marinated in a sweetened garlic sauce, then grilled and served topped with a hot chilli sauce.

4 medium-sized mackerel, cleaned and gutted
salt to taste
juice of 1 lemon

MARINADE
2 cloves garlic, crushed
2 tablespoons fish sauce or soya sauce
2 teaspoons dark brown sugar
1 teaspoon water

SAUCE
1 tablespoon melted butter
1 tablespoon soya sauce
½–1 small dried or fresh red chilli, seeded and finely chopped
1 small onion, finely chopped and fried brown in 1 tablespoon vegetable oil
coriander leaves to garnish

Dry the fish, score the skins two or three times with a sharp knife, season them with salt and sprinkle them with half the lemon juice. Combine the marinade ingredients in a shallow dish and add the fish. Brush the fish with the marinade and leave them to marinate for 30 minutes or longer. Line a grill pan with foil and oil the rack. Remove the fish from the marinade, arrange them on the grill rack and cook them under a hot grill for a total of 10 minutes, turning three to four times and basting them with any left-over marinade. Put the fish on a serving dish and pour a little melted butter over them. Quickly whisk together the sauce ingredients and pour them over the fish. Garnish with coriander leaves, and serve immediately.

Fish and Bulgar Wheat Kibbeh
Serves 4−6

Bulgar wheat is prepared by parboiling wholewheat grains in a minimum amount of water, then drying it in the sun and finally cracking it between stone rollers. Bulgar wheat is used in many Middle Eastern dishes, although perhaps the best known are tabbouleh and kibbeh. Kibbeh is made from bulgar wheat and lamb (or sometimes fish, as in this recipe) crushed together to form a mixture which is then spread on a tray and baked or formed into various shapes and deep-fried. Serve kibbeh with a green salad, yoghurt and pitta bread for a satisfying, unusual and nutritious meal. Use fillets of any white or oily fish in this dish.

12 oz (350 g) bulgar wheat (fine grade if available)
1 lb (450 g) white fish fillets, skinned
½ teaspoon ground coriander
grated zest of 1 small orange
2 medium onions, diced
salt and black pepper to taste
2 tablespoons vegetable oil
2 oz (50 g) pine nuts
2 oz (50 g) melted butter

Cover the bulgar wheat in cold water and soak for 20 minutes. Put the fish, coriander and orange zest in a blender or food processor and blend into a coarse paste. Lightly brown the onions in the oil, add the pine nuts and fry, stirring, for another minute. Preheat the oven to 175°C (350°F, gas mark 4). Drain the bulgar wheat and squeeze it dry. Mix together the fish paste and bulgar wheat, adding salt and pepper to taste, and then knead them together thoroughly by hand. Brush a shallow baking dish (about 10 x 8 in or 25 x 20 cm) with a little of the melted butter. Lay half the fish and bulgar wheat mixture in the bottom of the dish. Next spread a layer of the onion and pine nuts and then top this with the remaining fish and wheat mixture. Brush the top with the rest of melted butter and bake for 30 minutes or until golden brown.

Baked Fish in Tahini Sauce
Serves 4

This dish can be prepared with individual fillets of firm white fish (such as halibut, cod or haddock) or one large fish (such as sea bass, rainbow trout, salmon or grey mullet). Both methods are given, together with two recipes for tahini sauce. Sauce 1 contains less oil than sauce 2. Sauce 2 contains no garlic.

4 × 8 oz (225 g) fish fillets or
2 – 3 lb (900 g – 1.4 kg) whole fish, scaled, cleaned and washed
salt, black pepper and oil
vegetable oil for frying
juice of 1 lemon
2 tablespoons finely chopped fresh parsley
2 cloves garlic, crushed
2 tablespoons olive oil

TAHINI SAUCE 1
6 tablespoons (90 ml) tahini
3 tablespoons (45 ml) water or stock
1 tablespoon (15 ml) olive oil
2 cloves garlic
salt and black pepper to taste

TAHINI SAUCE 2
6 tablespoons (90 ml) tahini
3 tablespoons (45 ml) olive oil
1 tablespoon (15 ml) white wine vinegar
1 tablespoon (15 ml) water
salt and black pepper to taste

GARNISH
lettuce
lemon wedges
parsley sprigs
crushed cumin and coriander seeds
olives

Preheat oven to 350°F (175°C, gas mark 4).

TO BAKE FISH FILLETS

Cut out four pieces of foil each big enough to wrap an individual fillet and lightly oil them. Put one fillet on each piece of foil and sprinkle it with a quarter of the lemon juice, parsley, garlic and olive oil. Wrap up the foil and seal the edges. Bake in the oven for 20 – 25 minutes.

Mussels and Pasta (page 135)

Chicken Breasts with Lime (page 150)

TO BAKE WHOLE FISH

Make two or three incisions in the skin on both sides of the fish and then rub the fish inside and out with a mixture of salt, black pepper and oil. Set aside and leave for 1 hour. Cut out a piece of foil big enough to wrap the fish and lightly oil it. Put the fish in the foil and sprinkle over it the lemon juice, parsley, garlic and olive oil. Wrap up the foil and seal the edges. Bake in the oven for 25–30 minutes.

TO SERVE THE FISH

Combine all the ingredients for the tahini sauce (either version) and beat well together. If the sauce is too thick, add a little water. Gently heat the sauce through. Place the cooked fillets or whole fish on a bed of lettuce on a serving dish, surround with lemon wedges and olives. Pour the hot tahini dressing over the fish and decorate the dish with parsley sprigs and crushed cumin and coriander seeds. This dish can be served hot or cold.

VARIATION

Add lightly toasted or fried chopped almonds or pine nuts either to the sauce or to the ingredients which are sprinkled over the fish before baking.

Baked Fish with Hot Chilli and Tahini Sauce
Serves 4

Preheat oven to 175°C (350°F, gas mark 4). Prepare the whole fish or fish fillets as described in the recipe above but put them in a baking dish rather than wrapping them in foil. Prepare the tahini sauce (either version) and stir in ½ teaspoon hot chilli sauce or harissa. Pour the sauce over the fish or fillets in the baking dish. Cover and bake in the preheated oven for 20–30 minutes or until the fish or fillets are tender. Serve hot with lemon wedges and garnished with lightly fried or toasted pine nuts or almonds.

Chilled Baked Sea Bream
with Taratoor Sauce

Serves 4–6

Taratoor sauce is a Middle Eastern sauce made from toasted bread, pine nuts or almonds and the juice of baked fish. After baking, the fish is chilled before serving, and this dish is recommended for a summer meal or as the centrepiece of a cold buffet. For special occasions the fish is served filleted but 'whole', (see below).

2–3 lb (900 g–1.4 kg) whole sea bream, scaled, cleaned and washed
juice of 1 lemon
salt and black pepper
2 tablespoons olive oil

TARATOOR SAUCE
fish stock from the baked fish
2 slices bread, very lightly toasted and cut into small squares
2 cloves garlic, crushed
juice of 2 lemons
2 tablespoons olive oil
6 oz (175 g) pine nuts, lightly roasted
and/or chopped blanched almonds and/or ground almonds

GARNISH SUGGESTIONS
parsley sprigs
lemon wedges
olives
pine nuts or almonds, toasted
cucumber slices
apricot halves

Preheat the oven to 190°C (375°F, gas mark 4). Make two or three incisions in the skin on both sides of the fish and rub the fish inside and out with lemon juice. Sprinkle it with salt and black pepper and set aside for 1 hour. Oil a large baking dish, put the fish in it and pour over it the remaining oil. (If the fish is too big for the dish, cut the fish in two.) Cover and bake in the preheated oven for 25–30 minutes or until the flesh easily flakes on the thickest part of the fish. Do not overcook. Put the fish on a serving dish and chill. Reserve the cooking juices. Soak the toasted bread in these juices and combine this mixture in a blender (or pound together by hand) with the garlic, lemon juice, olive oil and nuts. Blend to a smooth cream, adding water if necessary. Pour the sauce over the chilled fish, smooth it out and decorate with a selection from the garnishings.

Taratoor sauce is sometimes made with tahini paste rather than pine nuts or almonds. Use the same amount of tahini instead of the nuts in the recipe.

Note: For special occasions this dish can be served in the traditional way. It takes a little time but is worth the effort. Cut the head and tail off the cooked, chilled fish. Skin the body and flake the flesh from the bones. Combine the flesh with a little diced onion and chopped parsley and season with salt and pepper. Arrange the flaked fish on the serving dish in its original shape. Cover it with taratoor sauce. Put the head and tail back in place and then have fun decorating your masterpiece with the garnishings suggested.

SHELLFISH

Vegetable and Shellfish Brown Rice Pilav
Serves 4

This dish is simple to prepare but combines all the elements of a demivegetarian diet in a nutritious and tasty way.

4 tablespoons olive oil
1 onion, peeled and chopped
6 oz (175 g) brown rice
1¼ pints (750 ml) chicken stock
freshly ground black pepper and salt to taste
2 tomatoes, diced
1 green or red pepper, seeded and diced
4 oz (100 g) fresh or frozen cooked peas
4 oz (100 g) peeled cooked prawns
½ pint (300 ml) fresh mussels in their shells, washed and scraped
chopped parsley to garnish

Heat the oil in a large frying pan and sauté the onion for 2 minutes. Then add the rice and cook for 2–3 minutes. Add the stock and seasoning. Bring to the boil and simmer for 35 minutes. Add the remaining ingredients, cover and cook for a further 5–10 minutes. Garnish with parsley.

Citrus Oysters
Serves 2–4

4 fresh oysters, opened
juice of ½ orange
1 tablespoon lemon juice
2 oz (50 g) wholemeal breadcrumbs
2 teaspoons grated orange rind
2 tablespoons chopped fresh chives
salt and freshly ground black pepper to taste
2 small eggs, beaten
extra grated orange rind to garnish

Remove the oysters from their shells, reserving the deeper shells for serving. Slice and poach the oysters for 3–4 minutes in the orange and lemon juice. Reserving 1 tablespoon breadcrumbs, stir the remaining breadcrumbs into the oysters with the orange rind and chives and season with salt and black pepper. Add the beaten eggs and stir over a gentle heat until the eggs are cooked. Divide the filling between the oyster shells and sprinkle the reserved breadcrumbs over the top. Flash the filled shells under the grill until the crumbs are crisp. Garnish with orange rind and serve.

Crab and Shrimp Bisque
Serves 4–6

A creamy, thick and filling soup which, served with bread and a salad, makes a perfect lunch. On its own it can be used as a delicious start to a meal.

1 oz (25 g) butter or polyunsaturated margarine
1 small onion, finely chopped
1 small clove garlic, crushed
1 stick celery, diced
¼ pint (150 ml) dry white wine
1 pint (550 ml) fish stock
1 bouquet garni
1 bay leaf
salt and freshly ground black pepper to taste
½ lb (225 g) shrimps, peeled
1 lb (450 g) brown and white crab meat
¼ pint (150 ml) single cream
1 tablespoon brandy
¼ pint (250 ml) natural yoghurt to garnish

Melt the butter or margarine in a large saucepan. Sauté the onion, garlic and celery until transparent. Add the wine, stock, bouquet garni, bay leaf and seasoning. Simmer for 5–10 minutes to allow the herbs to infuse. Stir in the shrimps, brown crab meat and half the white crab meat and simmer for 10 minutes. Liquidize, return to the heat and add the cream, brandy and remaining crab meat. Before serving swirl with natural yoghurt.

STIR-FRY SHELLFISH DISHES

Shellfish are quick to cook and lend themselves perfectly to stir-fry dishes. Here are two-stir fry recipes to try. In either of them squid or mussels, which are also convenient for stir-frying, could be substituted. Serve either dish with boiled brown or white rice.

Stir-Fry Scallops
Serves 2 as a main dish or 4 as a side dish

4 scallops
2 oz (50 g) flour
2 oz (50 g) butter or vegetable oil
1 small courgette, sliced
3 sticks celery, sliced
3 oz (75 g) carrots, cut into strips
3 oz (75 g) spring onions, chopped
salt and freshly ground black pepper to taste

Clean the scallops. Remove the coral, and if large, cut it into two or three pieces. Cut the white part into thin slices and coat both the coral pieces and the white slices with the flour. Melt the butter in a wok or frying pan and fry the scallops gently for 3 minutes. Add the courgette and the celery and fry for a further 2 minutes. Add the carrots and spring onions, fry until just tender, season to taste, and serve immediately.

Note: For the scallops you may substitute 8 oz (225 g) thinly sliced prepared squid or mussels.

Stir-Fry Prawns
Serves 4

1 tablespoon vegetable oil
1 clove garlic, crushed
1 medium onion, thinly sliced
1 in (2.5 cm) root ginger, thinly sliced
2 medium carrots, cut in matchsticks
1 green pepper, seeded and cut into thin strips
2 oz (50 g) Chinese leaves, shredded
2 oz (50 g) beansprouts
12 oz (350 g) peeled prawns
1 tablespoon soya sauce

Heat the oil in a wok or large frying pan. Fry the garlic, onion and ginger, stirring all the time. Once the onion is softened add the carrots and green pepper and stir-fry for 2 minutes. Then stir in the Chinese leaves and beansprouts. After 1 minute add the prawns and soya sauce. Stir-fry for a further 2 minutes and then serve immediately.

Note: Substitute 1 lb (450 g) thinly sliced prepared squid or mussels for the prawns if your wish. Add the squid to the wok or frying pan at the same time as the carrots and green pepper.

Prawn and Cottage Cheese Soufflé
Serves 2–4

A light, low-fat, high-protein soufflé.

½ oz (15 g) butter or polyunsaturated margarine
½ oz (15 g) plain flour
¼ pint (150 ml) milk
salt and freshly ground black pepper to taste
2 medium eggs, separated
2 oz (50 g) cottage cheese (with chives if you wish)
½ lb (225 g) cooked peeled prawns, rinsed
1 tablespoon fresh chopped parsley

Preheat the oven to 180°C (350°F, gas mark 4) and butter a 1½ pint (850 ml) soufflé dish. Melt the butter in a saucepan, stir in the flour and cook for 1 minute. Remove from the heat. Gradually add the milk. Stir over a gentle heat until the sauce thickens, then season with salt and black pepper. Beat in the egg yolks. Stir in the cottage cheese, prawns (reserving 1 tablespoon for garnish) and parsley. Whisk the egg whites until stiff but not dry, and fold them into the mixture. Pour the mixture into the soufflé dish, and sprinkle the reserved prawns over the top. Bake for 30–35 minutes until well risen and golden brown. Serve immediately.

Mussels and Pasta

Serves 4

A delicious pasta dish in which tagliatelle is served with mussels and a tomato sauce.

4 pints (2.25 litres) fresh mussels
1 medium onion, chopped
parsley sprigs
½ pint (275 ml) fish stock, water or white wine
12 oz (350 g) green or plain tagliatelle

SAUCE
1 tablespoon sunflower or other vegetable oil
1 small onion, finely chopped
2 cloves garlic, crushed
1 × 14 oz (400 g) tin chopped tomatoes
2 oz (50 g) button mushrooms, sliced
2 tablespoons fresh mixed herbs, chopped
large pinch sugar
salt and freshly ground black pepper to taste

Scrub the mussels, removing the beards and discarding any that are open. Place them in a large pan with the onion, parsley and stock water or wine. Cover and steam until they open (about 5 minutes). Discard any that have not opened and reserve the cooking liquor. Cook the pasta in a large pan of boiling water. While it is cooking, heat the oil and fry the onion and garlic until soft and transparent. Stir in the tomatoes, mushrooms, herbs, sugar, salt and pepper, and add ½ pint (275 ml) of the reserved liquor. Bring to the boil and simmer until the sauce is thickened and reduced (about 10 minutes). Remove the mussel meat from the shells and add it to the sauce. Drain the pasta and combine it with mussels and tomato sauce.

Moules à la Bordelaise
Serves 4

Bordelaise simply means 'in the manner of Bordeaux', so this dish may have originated in that area of France, or perhaps the cook that devised it used Bordeaux wine in its preparation. Whatever, it is simple to make and tasty.

4 pints (2.5 litres) fresh mussels, washed and scrubbed
4 fl oz (100 ml) dry white wine
1 oz (25 g) butter
1 medium onion, finely chopped
1 clove garlic, crushed
1 lb (450 g) fresh tomatoes, skinned, seeded and chopped
3 tablespoons fresh parsely, chopped
rind of 1/2 lemon
salt and freshly ground black pepper to taste
3 oz (75 g) fresh brown breadcrumbs
melted butter

Place the mussels and wine in a large pan, cover and set over a high heat until they have opened. Strain the mussels and remove the shells, reserving the cooking liquor. Melt the butter and sauté the onion and garlic for 2 minutes. Add the tomatoes, parsley, lemon, salt and black pepper, and enough reserved liquor to enable the tomatoes to simmer until cooked. Arrange the mussels in a gratin dish. Pour the sauce (which should be quite thin) over the mussels and sprinkle them with the breadcrumbs. Dribble a little butter over the top and pop them under a moderate grill until golden.

CHICKEN

In recent years the popularity of chicken has increased, while our consumption of red meat has declined. Nowadays chicken is an economical ingredient as well as being a convenient and versatile one. With its high protein and low saturated-fat content, plus moderate amounts of thiamine, riboflavin and nicotinic acid of the vitamin B complex, chicken can make a substantial contribution to a healthy diet. The health-giving qualities of chicken can be negated by the way the birds are reared, but fortunately, because of consumer pressure, more producers are keeping their birds in better conditions and this is a trend we should all support.

TYPES OF CHICKEN

Oven-ready chickens are sold completely eviscerated, normally chilled, with or without giblets.

Frozen chicken is first cleaned and then quickly frozen. It is a convenient way of buying chicken because it can be kept in the home freezer until required.

Poussins are 4–6 weeks old and weigh about 1 lb (0.5 kg). They are available fresh or frozen. One bird is enough for one large or two small portions.

Cornfed chickens are reared on a diet of maize grains which gives the birds a distinctive yellow hue. They are predominantly avialable fresh, though some are frozen.

Boiling fowl are available in a number of retail outlets. These are smaller, less meaty birds, usually weighing 2½–3½ lb, (1.5–1.6 kg).

BUYING ADVICE

When buying fresh poultry, check the sell-by date carefully and make sure the bird is free from bruising or any other damage. If you are not certain of your own prowess in choosing for quality, go to a reputable retailer. Always look for 'Grade A' quality chicken or products with the Quality British Chicken mark.

STORAGE

When storing frozen whole chicken or frozen chicken portions, follow the instructions on the pack.

Fresh whole chickens and fresh chicken portions often carry storage instructions on the pack. If they do not, they should always be kept in the refrigerator and cooked within two days of purchase. If they are in a pack, the seal should be broken to allow the chicken to breathe.

Ready-cooked chicken should also be refrigerated and eaten within three days or, if stuffed, within two days.

Recommended freezer storage periods	
Frozen whole chicken	3 months
Frozen chicken portions	3 months
Cooked chicken	2 months
Giblets	3 months
Boiling fowl	9 months

Ready-frozen poultry should be put in the home freezer as soon as possible to prevent it from thawing. No poultry should ever be refrozen.

THAWING

Frozen chicken must be thoroughly thawed, preferably in its bag with the seal punctured, prior to cooking. Ideally chicken should be thawed in the refrigerator to ensure that it stays as fresh as possible. In the case of whole chicken, this means planning ahead.

The following are recommended thawing times for frozen whole chicken.

Weight	Thawing at room temperature	Thawing in refrigerator
2 lb (1 kg)	8 hours	28 hours
3 lb (1.25 kg)	9 hours	32 hours
4 lb (2.5 kg)	14 hours	50 hours
7 lb (3 kg)	16 hours	56 hours

Always ensure that chicken is thoroughly defrosted before cooking otherwise it will not cook all the way through. Make sure there are no ice crystals in the cavity and the legs and thighs are soft and flexible.

COOKING

The average cooking time for roast chicken is 20 minutes to the pound plus 20 minutes at 190°C (375°F, gas mark 5).

The use of foil (dull side uppermost) helps to retain the bird's natural juices and reduces the need for basting, but a foil-wrapped bird will require slightly longer cooking time (for an average 3½ lb (1.6 kg) bird an extra 12−15 minutes). Remove the foil for the last 20 minutes to allow the bird to brown. To test when your chicken is cooked, insert a skewer into the thickest part of the thigh. When the juices run out clear, then the bird is cooked.

ALTERNATIVE COOKING METHODS

Microwaving: Chicken can be both defrosted and cooked in a microwave. However, as oven models vary, it is most important to check carefully the manufacturer's instructions before proceeding.

Pressure cooking: Pressure cooking is a quick and economical method of cooking chicken but, again, as cooker models vary, you must check the instructions for your particular model. As the cooking time is calculated from the weight, you must include the weight of any stuffing. However, if you are cooking portions of chicken you do not have to increase the cooking time, even if you are cooking eight rather than four portions.

Slow cooking: Slow cookers are extremely useful – they enable you to go out all day and come back to a ready-cooked meal. Make sure the chicken is completely thawed and always cook whole birds on the high setting.

Chicken bricks: Chicken bricks are a popular way of cooking poultry because the bird cooks in its natural juices, so no added fat is required and the flavour and nutrients are retained. Soak your chicken brick in water for 15 minutes before you use it. As soon as you switch on the oven, set the temperature to 140°C (275°F, gas mark 1) and put the chicken brick in the oven for 5 minutes. Then place your chicken in the brick, put it back into the oven and set the dial to the required cooking temperature.

Roasting bags: Roasting bags keep the oven clean and brown the poultry really well. Flour the inside of the roasting bag before cooking, as this helps the self-basting. Make slits in the bag before putting the chicken in the oven to prevent the bag exploding.

KITCHEN HYGIENE AND CHICKEN

Store uncooked or defrosting chicken in a container and do not allow blood or other juices to drip onto other food. Wash your hands before and after dealing with the chicken or chicken joints and use different cutting boards for cooked and raw food. Make sure all utensils and work surfaces are very clean. Hygiene experts now recommend non-wooden chopping boards for cutting up raw food.

Pot-Roast Chicken Joints
Serves 4

A very simple, very British casserole dish which is usually enjoyed by all the family.

1 lb (450 g) carrots
1 lb (450 g) onions
4 chicken joints (legs or breasts or chicken quarters)
1 lb (450 g) small fresh tomatoes or drained tinned tomatoes
2 teaspoons fresh rosemary or 1 teaspoon dried rosemary
2 oz (50 g) butter
salt and black pepper to taste
¼ pint (150 ml) dry cider

Scrape the carrots and cut them into chunks; peel the onions and cut them into thick rounds. Preheat the oven to 180°C (350°F, gas mark 4). Lightly grease a deep casserole and place the chicken, carrots, onions and tomatoes in the bottom. Mix the butter and seasoning and place them in the casserole. Pour the cider over the chicken and cover the casserole tightly. Bake in the preheated oven for 1 hour or until the chicken is tender. Remove the lid for the last 10–15 minutes to brown the skin. Lift out the chicken with a slotted spoon and place it on a serving dish. Surround it with the strained vegetables. Serve the gravy separately.

Note: For extra flavour add 1 teaspoon juniper berries to the pot.

Rice and Chicken Onepot

Serves 4

A simple one-pot meal. Once you become familiar with making this dish you can put all the ingredients together, set it to simmer and forget about it for 30 minutes. It is fine served on its own or with a plain green salad.

4 chicken thighs
2 tablespoons vegetable oil
6 oz (175 g) long-grain white rice
1 pint (600 ml) chicken stock
8 oz (225 g) tomatoes, cut into quarters
2 garlic cloves, peeled and crushed
7 oz (200 g) sweetcorn
salt and freshly ground black pepper to taste
4 oz (100 g) shelled peas (fresh or frozen)

In a deep pan or casserole fry the chicken joints in the oil for 5 to 6 minutes until evenly browned on all sides. Add the rice and fry gently for 1 minute, stirring continuously, until it is opaque. Add the chicken stock, tomatoes, garlic, sweetcorn, salt and pepper. Cover and simmer gently for about 30 minutes until the chicken and rice are tender. Add the peas and simmer for a further 5 minutes or until all the liquid has been absorbed. Check the moisture content of the pan and either add a little water if the rice is dry or leave the pan lid off for a while to reduce the liquid if it is too wet.

Note: If using brown rice, soak it for a couple of hours before use and increase the initial simmering period in the recipe to 40−45 minutes.

Chicken Breasts Stuffed with Leek, Cheese and Pine Nuts
Serves 4

If you look at a chicken breast carefully you will see along one edge a line of skin that, if cut open, reveals a natural pouch in the breast that is perfect for stuffing. Cut the pouch open, widen it with your knife, then fill it with the stuffing and secure it with a cocktail stick. This recipe uses a demiveg stuffing mixture of leek, cheese and pine nuts flavoured with parsley and lemon juice. With the chicken, the mixture makes a nutritious food combination low in fat and high in protein. Serve hot with baked potatoes and seasonal vegetables.

4 chicken breasts
1 tablespoon sunflower or other vegetable oil
1 leek, trimmed, washed and finely sliced
3 tablespoons fresh brown breadcrumbs
1 tablespoon pine nuts (or sunflower seeds)
1 egg yolk
1 tablespoon finely chopped fresh parsley
salt and freshly ground black pepper to taste
3 oz (75 g) Gouda or Edam cheese, grated
juice and finely grated rind of ½ lemon
watercress to garnish

Preheat the oven to 200°C (400°F, gas mark 6). Skin the chicken breasts and cut a pocket in each as described above. Heat the oil in a pan and sauté the leek for 2 minutes. Remove the pan from the heat. Add the breadcrumbs, pine nuts, egg yolk, parsley, seasoning and cheese. Mix in the lemon juice and rind. Fill each chicken breast evenly with the mixture and secure each with a cocktail stick. Bake the stuffed breasts in a greased ovenproof dish in the preheated oven for 35−40 minutes.

Baked Chicken Drumsticks in
Peanut Sauce
Serves 4

Like the chicken satay recipe (see p. 154) this recipe uses a peanut sauce but the method is simple and quicker. Drumsticks served in this way make a convenient hot buffet dish or a quick but interesting meal served with baked potatoes and a salad.

4 large or 8 small chicken drumsticks
½ lemon
salt and freshly ground black pepper
3 tablespoons crunchy peanut butter
1 tablespoon soya sauce
2 tablespoons chicken stock or water
1–2 tablespoons finely chopped unsalted peanuts

GARNISH
fresh coriander or parsley
lemon or lime wedges

Preheat the oven to 190°C (375°F, gas mark 5). Make small cuts in the chicken drumsticks. Rub them all over with lemon and season with salt and pepper. Put the peanut butter into a pan with the soya sauce and chicken stock or water and heat gently until well blended. Place the drumsticks in a shallow ovenproof dish, spoon the peanut butter mixture evenly over each drumstick and sprinkle them with chopped peanuts. Bake in the preheated oven for 25–30 minutes, depending on size. Serve hot garnished with coriander or parsley and wedges of lemon or lime.

Barbecued Chicken Drumsticks in Foil
Serves 4–8

Drumsticks are most convenient for cooking out of doors and they can be eaten without a knife and fork. In this recipe the drumsticks are wrapped in foil with flavourings and chopped courgettes and then grilled. They retain all their flavour and moisture and the method provides a neat parcel of food for each person.

8 drumsticks
2 fl oz (50 ml) olive oil
8 small courgettes, chopped into ½ in (1 cm) rings
4 cloves garlic, finely chopped
salt and black pepper to taste
2 teaspoons fresh basil or 1 teaspoon dried basil
2 teaspoons sugar
1 tablespoon tomato purée

Chicken and Apple Stir-Fry (page 152)

Rhubarb and Ginger Flummery (page 169)

Prepare a charcoal grill. Brush the drumsticks with oil and grill for about 2 minutes on each side. Cut eight squares of cooking foil, each one big enough to take a drumstick. Put one drumstick on each square and scatter around it a portion of the courgette rings. Sprinkle garlic, salt and black pepper, basil and sugar over the top and dab each one with a little tomato purée. Wrap the foil round the drumsticks to form a parcel and cook the parcels over the charcoal fire for about 10 minutes each side.

Note: The foil parcels can also be baked if it is more convenient. Lay them on an oiled roasting tin and bake for about 25 minutes in a preheated oven at 200°C (400°F, gas mark 6).

Chicken and Lettuce Ball Kebabs
Serves 4

These kebabs can be grilled or barbecued. The recipe looks a little difficult but once you have minced the chicken (two boneless chicken breasts provide enough meat) it is quite simple to follow and the finished kebabs look very professional and taste delicious. Serve very hot with salad and rice.

1 lb (450 g) minced chicken
2 oz (50 g) red pepper, seeded and finely chopped
2 teaspoons Worcestershire sauce
salt and freshly ground black pepper to taste
2 egg yolks
3 oz (75 g) lettuce, finely chopped
4 tablespoons finely chopped parsley
2 oz (50 g) sesame seeds
olive oil
curly endive to garnish

Mix the minced chicken with the chopped red pepper, Worcestershire sauce, salt and pepper, and egg yolks. Mix in the chopped lettuce. Mould the mixture into small balls about the size of a small plum. Roll half the balls in chopped parsley and half in sesame seeds. Chill for 2 hours. Carefully thread alternate balls on kebab skewers and brush clean lightly with oil. Grill over a preheated barbecue or under a conventional grill until golden brown and tender, turning once or twice during cooking. Serve garnished with leaves of curly endive.

Grilled Chicken Kebabs
Serves 4

Chicken, once it has been boned, is excellent for making kebabs. Chicken breasts are the easiest part of the bird to bone. If you cannot do it yourself your butcher or poulterer will do it for you, but it is not difficult and all you need is a small sharp knife and the patience to cut around the bone until you can pull it free. A number of supermarkets now sell fresh and frozen boneless chicken breasts.

In this recipe, lean chicken pieces are marinated in yoghurt flavoured with lemon rind, then threaded on skewers with red and green peppers and mushrooms, and grilled. Serve the kebabs on a bed of rice or with pitta bread and salad.

4 chicken breasts, skinned and boned and cut into walnut-size pieces
1/2 pint (300 ml) natural yoghurt
grated rind and juice of 1 lemon
1 tablespoon finely chopped parsley
1 red pepper and 1 green pepper or 2 red peppers or
2 green peppers, seeded and cut into 1 in (2.5 cm) squares
4 oz (100 g) button mushrooms, washed

Put the chicken into a bowl with half the yoghurt and the lemon rind. Mix well to coat each piece of chicken in yoghurt. Cover and leave in the refrigerator for 4 hours or longer. Combine the remaining yoghurt, lemon juice and parsley in a small bowl, cover and put in the refrigerator also.

When you are ready to cook the kebabs remove the chicken and sauce from the fridge. Thread the chicken with alternating pieces of red pepper, green pepper and mushroom on four skewers (wooden ones are best). Line the base of the grill pan with cooking foil. Put the kebabs in the grill pan and brush them with the marinade. Grill them under a moderate heat for about 15 minutes, turning and brushing them with the marinade every now and again. Serve them with the yoghurt, parsley and lemon sauce and any leftover marinade.

Note: The kebabs may also be cooked over a charcoal grill.

Simmered Chicken Stuffed with Wild Rice
Serves 6

Wild rice is a cereal grain native to North America. It belongs to the same broad family as the rice plant. It is a very beautiful plant which grows in areas of abundant fresh water. The Red Indians would collect the grass from canoes by floating alongside the ripe plants and then gently pulling them over the sides of the boat and knocking the delicately held grains into the hull. The plant is difficult to grow domestically and is consequently expensive. Nutritionally it is very rich and contains more protein and vitamins than regular rice. Raw wild rice is brown, but it acquires a faint purplish colour when cooked. It has a delicate nutty flavour. A wild rice mixture is used in this recipe to stuff a chicken before cooking. You could of course use plain white or brown rice but the wild rice gives the dish a special flavour. The chicken is simmered in stock or water flavoured with apricots and caraway seeds.

9 oz (275 g) cooked wild rice
2 tablespoons sultanas
salt and freshly ground black pepper to taste
2 tablespoons olive oil
1 small onion, finely chopped
1 clove garlic, crushed
1 red pepper, seeded and chopped
3½ lb (1.5 kg) chicken, prepared for cooking
8 oz (225 g) dried apricots (sun-dried if possible)
1 teaspoon caraway seeds
chicken stock or water

Mix the wild rice with the sultanas and salt and pepper. Heat the oil and fry the onion gently for 3 minutes, then add the garlic and red pepper and fry gently for a further 3 minutes. Stir the onion mixture into the rice. Stuff the chicken with the rice and onion stuffing and seal the opening as tightly as possible with wooden cocktail sticks or skewers. Put the chicken in a large pan with the dried apricots and caraway seeds and season with salt and pepper. Add sufficient chicken stock or water to come about halfway up the chicken. Cover and bring to the boil. Reduce the heat and simmer for 1½ hours or until the chicken is just tender. (The apricots will form a thickish sauce as they cook. Use this to baste the chicken during cooking).

Country Chicken Casserole
Serves 4–6

A straightforward, simple, nutritious, simple, family recipe, quick and enjoyable to prepare.

*3½ lb (1.6 kg) chicken, prepared for cooking
8 oz (225 g) young carrots, peeled
8 small onions
2 sticks celery, chopped
4 potatoes, peeled and halved
2 bay leaves
parsley sprigs
¼ pint (150 ml) red wine
¼ pint (150 ml) chicken stock or water
salt and black pepper to taste*

Preheat the oven to 170°C (325°F, gas mark 3). Put the chicken into a casserole dish with all the other ingredients, season and cover. Cook the chicken for about 2 hours or until it is tender and the meat cooked through. Cut the chicken into pieces and serve with the vegetables.

Honey-Roasted Chicken
Serves 4–6

This method produces a sweet golden-brown chicken complemented by a garnishing of chopped ginger and almonds.

*3½ lb (1.6 kg) oven-ready chicken, cleaned and wiped dry
1 lemon
salt
2 oz (50 g) butter
2 tablespoons honey*

GARNISH (OPTIONAL)
*chopped preserved ginger
chopped almonds*

Preheat the oven to 230°C (450°F, gas mark 8). Cut the lemon in half and rub the chicken inside and out with one of the halves. Sprinkle the chicken inside and out with salt. Melt the butter and whisk it into the honey together with the juice of the remaining half of the lemon. Brush the chicken inside and out with this mixture. Put the chicken in a well-oiled roasting pan and place it in the oven. Reduce the heat after 10 minutes to 80°C (350°F, gas mark 4) and then cook for about 20 minutes per pound (450 g) of bird. Baste occasionally during cooking. Serve the chicken jointed and garnished with preserved ginger and chopped almonds. To reduce the cooking time, joint the chicken before roasting.

Curried Roasted Chicken
Serves 4–6

This is nothing like the ubiquitous (but sometimes delicious) chicken curry sold in Indian restaurants. The curry powder is made into a paste and rubbed into the chicken before roasting, imparting a mild flavour that permeates the whole chicken.

3½ lb (1.6 kg) oven-ready chicken, cleaned and wiped dry
salt
4 oz (100 g) butter, melted
juice of 1 lemon
1 teaspoon thyme
1 teaspoon curry powder
¼ teaspoon cayenne
½ teaspoon nutmeg
salt and black pepper to taste

Preheat the oven to 230°C (450°F, gas mark 8). Sprinkle the outside and inside of the chicken with salt. Combine the remaining ingredients, using only half the butter, and mix them into a smooth paste. Rub this into the chicken inside and out. Put the remaining butter in a roasting pan and place it in the oven for a few minutes. Now put the chicken in the pan and return it to the oven. Reduce the heat after 10 minutes to 180 °C (350°F, gas mark 4) and then cook for about 20 minutes per pound (450 g) of chicken until tender. During cooking baste the chicken occasionally with the pan juices. To reduce the cooking time the chicken can be jointed before roasting.

VARIATION

For golden-brown chicken follow the recipe above but substitute ½ teaspoon saffron powder and 1 teaspoon turmeric for the curry powder, cayenne and nutmeg.

Chicken Breasts with Lime
Serves 4

Limes are now available all year round and are worth trying in many recipes as a change from lemons. Their flavour is generally slightly sharper than that of the lemon. This recipe is uncomplicated but produces a very flavoursome chicken dish.

1 medium onion, thinly sliced
2 tablespoons olive oil
1 clove garlic, crushed
4 chicken breasts, skinned (and boned if you wish)
grated zest and juice of 1 lime
salt and freshly ground black pepper to taste
8 fl oz (225 ml) chicken stock
lime wedges to garnish

Fry the onion gently in the olive oil for 3 minutes. Add the garlic and the chicken breasts and fry until the chicken is evenly coloured. Add the lime zest and juice, salt and pepper and the stock. Cover and simmer gently for 20 minutes or until the chicken is tender. Remove the chicken to a serving dish and keep it warm in the oven. Liquidize the sauce and reheat it gently. Spoon the sauce over the cooked chicken breasts. Serve garnished with lime wedges. Squeeze juice from the wedges over the chicken before eating.

Chicken Breasts with Mustard
Serves 4

This is perhaps the simplest recipe in the book but it is nevertheless effective and worth trying with different types of mustard. I prefer to use a wholegrain coarse mustard which is not as strong as traditional English mustard, although the latter appeals to some tastes. Serve with rice or chipped potatoes.

4 chicken breasts with skin on
4 full teaspoons prepared or ready-made mustard
6 fl oz (175 ml) single cream

Preheat the oven to 190°C (375°F, gas mark 5). Lightly butter a baking dish. Spread the chicken breasts with the mustard, place them in the dish and bake them in the oven for 25–30 minutes or until tender. Transfer the breasts to a warmed serving dish. Spoon the juices and sticky bits from the baking dish into a small pan, add the cream and stir with a fork until it starts to boil. Immediately pour the sauce over the chicken and serve.

STIR-FRIED CHICKEN DISHES

Stir-frying is a quick and versatile method of making a one-pot meal. A wok is the best pan to use for stir-frying because its shape concentrates the heat on the food and cooks it quickly and evenly; however, you can also use a deep frying pan and still get good results. The secret of good stir-frying is to make sure you cut all the ingredients into mouthsize pieces and to stir constantly during cooking. Here are two distinctive stir-fry chicken recipes.

Stir-Fry Chicken and Cashew Nuts
Serves 4

3 tablespoons vegetable oil
2 or 3 chicken breasts, skinned, boned and cut into thin strips
4 spring onions, chopped
1 teaspoon finely chopped fresh root ginger
1 large clove garlic, finely chopped
2 tablespoons cashew nuts
4 oz (100 g) beansprouts, washed and dried
salt and freshly ground black pepper to taste
1 tablespoon soya sauce
3 tablespoons dry sherry
1 tablespoon finely chopped parsley
lime wedges to garnish

Heat the vegetable oil in a wok or a deep frying pan. Add the chicken strips, spring onions, ginger and garlic and stir-fry for about 5 minutes. Add the cashew nuts, beansprouts, salt and pepper, and stir-fry for a further 1–2 minutes. Add the sherry, soya sauce and parsley and stir-fry for a further minute. Turn onto a serving dish and garnish with wedges of lime.

Chicken and Apple Stir-Fry
Serves 4

3 tablespoons vegetable oil
1 clove garlic, crushed
2 or 3 chicken breasts, skinned, boned and cut into thin strips
1 green pepper, seeded and cut into thin strips
1 red pepper, seeded and cut into thin strips
2 oz (50 g) mangetout, topped and tailed
finely grated rind and juice of 1/2 lemon
4 oz (100 g) fresh beansprouts, washed and dried
2 tablespoons chopped parsley
1 tablespoon light soya sauce
2 crisp eating apples, peeled, cored and diced

Heat the oil in a wok or large frying pan. Add the garlic and sauté for 2 minutes. Add the chicken strips and toss continuously until they are sealed on both sides. Add peppers and mangetout and stir-fry for a further 2 minutes. Add the remaining ingredients and stir-fry for a further 1–2 minutes. Serve immediately.

Chicken Chilli Beans
Serves 4–6

This dish is like chilli con carne with chicken instead of beef. It is a useful way of using up leftover cooked chicken. Chicken and beans make a very nutritious combination.

1 tablespoon vegetable oil
1 medium onion, chopped
2 cloves garlic, crushed
1–2 teaspoons hot pepper sauce
1/2 teaspoon ground cumin
1/2 teaspoon ground coriander
1/2 teaspoon dried oregano
1/2 teaspoon dried basil
8 oz (225 g) cooked chicken, diced
14 oz (400 g) tinned tomatoes, drained, reserving the juice
1 teaspoon honey
8 oz (225 g) dried red kidney beans, soaked, cooked and drained, or
1 lb (450 g) tinned red beans, drained
2 tablespoons bulgar wheat (optional)
salt and black pepper to taste

Heat the oil in a saucepan, add the onion and garlic and sauté until golden. Add the hot pepper sauce, cumin, coriander, oregano, basil and chicken pieces. Sauté together for 2–3 minutes and then add the drained tomatoes, half the tomato juice and honey. Cover the pan and simmer for 5 minutes. Add the kidney beans and bulgar wheat if used. If the mixture is not moist enough add the remaining tomato juice. Season with salt and black pepper. Add more hot pepper sauce if you like it spicy. Cover the pan and simmer for 10 minutes. Grated cheese can be sprinkled over the top as an extra treat.

Chicken Gratin
Serves 4

This recipe requires cooked portions of chicken. These may be bought ready cooked or you can simply cook chicken portions in a lightly buttered roasting tin in a medium oven for 25–30 minutes. The cooked chicken is then lightly baked in a tomato-flavoured white sauce topped with grated cheese.

1 oz (25 g) butter
6 oz (175 g) button mushrooms, sliced
4 shallots, peeled and finely chopped
1 oz (25 g) plain flour
8 fl oz (225 ml) milk
1 lb (450 g) tomatoes, skinned and chopped, or
14 oz (400 g) tin tomatoes drained and chopped
salt and black pepper to taste
2 teaspoons fresh tarragon or 1 teaspoon dried tarragon (optional)
4 cooked chicken portions (legs or breasts), skinned
2 oz (50 g) Red Leicester cheese, grated

Preheat the oven to 200°C (400°F, gas mark 6). Melt the butter in a saucepan and add the mushrooms and shallots. Sauté gently without browning. Stir in the flour and milk and mix thoroughly. Bring to the boil, stirring continuously. Lower the heat, stir in the tomatoes, salt and pepper, and tarragon if used. Cover and simmer gently for 5 minutes. Place the chicken portions in an ovenproof dish, pour the sauce over them and sprinkle the cheese on top. Bake for 20–30 minutes until cheese has melted and browned.

Chicken Satay
Serves 6–8

Chicken pieces are marinated in a curry-flavoured marinade, then threaded onto skewers, grilled and served with a spicy hot peanut sauce (see below). Chicken satay is a popular street food in Southeast Asia. Serve it as a starter, part of a barbecue or buffet, or as a main dish with boiled rice and cucumber salad sauce (see below).

3 cloves garlic, finely chopped
2 teaspoons finely grated ginger root
2 teaspoons curry powder
1 teaspoon turmeric
1 teaspoon ground coriander
5 fl oz (1 ml) tinned coconut milk or cows' milk
4 chicken breasts, boned and cut into 1 × ¼ (2.5 × 0.75 cm)

Combine the garlic, ginger root, curry powder, turmeric, coriander and coconut or cows' milk and beat well together. Put this marinade into a large bowl and add the chicken pieces. Make sure each piece is coated in the marinade. Cover the bowl and set aside in the refrigerator for 2 or more hours. During this time prepare the peanut and cucumber sauces (see below). At the end of the 2 hours thread the chicken strips onto bamboo or metal skewers, leaving space at either end to hold the skewer. Preheat a hot grill or barbecue fire and grill the chicken over or under the flame, close to the heat, for 2–3 minutes each side. During this time baste the satay with any left over marinade. During the grilling or barbecuing process aim to get the distance and heat just right so that the finished satay is speckled with dark brown singe marks. Serve with peanut and cucumber sauces. Dip the chicken satay in one or both sauces before eating.

Cucumber Sauce
Serves 4

This is more a salad than a sauce, but served with hot chilli dishes or with satay dishes it is cool and refreshing.

1 tablespoon cider vinegar or rice vinegar
2 tablespoons sugar
2 tablespoons hot water
½ teaspoon salt
½ medium cucumber, thinly sliced
½ small onion, thinly sliced

Put the vinegar, sugar, hot water and salt into a small bowl and stir until the sugar dissolves completely. Arrange the cucumber slices on a serving dish and pour the vinegar mixture over them. Decorate the top with onion slices. Chill and serve.

Peanut Butter Sauce
Makes ½ pint (275 ml)

Peanut butter sauce usually accompanies satay dishes, but it is also good as a dipping sauce with raw vegetables or as a side dish with meat or chicken dishes.

8 fl oz (225 ml) tinned coconut milk or 2 oz (50 g) creamed coconut
dissolved in 6 fl oz (175 ml) hot water
1 teaspoon curry powder
2 tablespoons smooth peanut butter
1 tablespoon sugar
1 tablespoon lemon juice
1 tablespoon fish sauce or soya sauce
salt to taste

Heat the coconut milk in a saucepan over a low heat. Stir in the curry powder and then add the other ingredients. Stirring continuously, bring the sauce to the boil. Reduce the eat and simmer, uncovered, for 5 minutes. It is now ready to serve.

Chicken Blintzes
Serves 6

A blintz is a filled pancake roll that is fried or baked in a little butter until crisp and brown. This recipe uses a chicken filling, although cheese or fruit fillings are more common. Piping hot, golden-brown blintzes are difficult for anyone to resist.

BATTER
3 oz (75 g) plain sifted flour
3 medium-sized eggs
3/4 pint (450 ml) milk
1/2 teaspoon salt

FILLING
1 tablespoon vegetable oil
1 large onion, diced
1 green pepper, seeded and diced
1 clove garlic, crushed
10 oz (275 g) cooked chicken, shredded
1 tablespoon plain flour
3/4 pint (450 ml) chicken stock
salt and black pepper to taste
2 tablespoons chopped fresh parsley
butter for frying and for greasing the baking dish

TO MAKE THE BATTER
Put all the batter ingredients into a mixing bowl or an electric blender and beat until smooth. Set the batter aside and chill for 1 hour or more.

TO MAKE THE FILLING
Heat the oil in a saucepan and add the onion. Sauté, stirring for 1 minute, then add the green pepper and garlic and sauté for another minute. Stir in the chicken and sprinkle the flour over the top. Stir the flour into the mixture and sauté for 1 minute more. Pour the chicken stock into the pan, season with salt and black pepper, stir well and bring to the boil. Reduce the heat, cover and simmer for 10 minutes. Stir in the parsley and remove the pan from the heat.

TO MAKE THE PANCAKES
Heat 1/4 teaspoon butter over a medium flame in a 6 in (15 cm) frying pan (a crêpes pan is best) until it just sizzles. Then pour in about 2 1/2 tablespoons batter and spread it evenly over the base of the pan. Fry the pancake for about 1 minute on each side or until just browned. Stack the pancakes on a plate and repeat the process until all the batter is used up (about 18 pancakes).

TO FILL AND BAKE THE PANCAKES

Preheat the oven to 220°C (425°F, gas mark 7). Put a heaped spoonful of filling into the centre of a pancake, wrap one edge over it and then roll the pancake up, tucking in the edges as you go to seal in the filling. Repeat for all the pancakes and filling. Butter a large shallow baking dish and lay the blintzes inside in one layer. Brush the tops with some melted butter and bake them in the preheated oven for about 20 minutes. Serve immediately.

Rice, Orange and Chicken Pilav

Serves 4–6

This Arab dish takes simple ingredients and converts them into a colourful dish of subtle flavours.

2–3 lb (900 g–1.4 kg) boiling chicken, cut into 6 pieces
1½ pints (850 ml) water
salt to taste
2 medium onions, thinly sliced
8 oz (225 g) carrots, thinly sliced
4 tablespoons butter or oil
peel of 1 orange, shredded (reserve orange for garnish)
1 teaspoon ground cardamom
1 teaspoon ground cinnamon
½ teaspoon turmeric or saffron
8 oz (225 g) long-grain rice
salt and black pepper to taste

Put the chicken pieces in a saucepan, add the water and salt and bring to the boil. Skim off any foam that forms, reduce the heat, cover the pot and simmer until the chicken pieces are almost tender but not to the point where the meat is falling off the bones. Remove the chicken from the pan and cut off the lean meat. Discard the fat, skin and bones. Reserve the stock. In a large frying pan sauté the onions and carrots in the butter or oil until the onions start to brown. Stir in the orange peel spices and rice and season with salt and black pepper. Stir and fry for 2 minutes. Put the chicken pieces in the bottom of a saucepan and cover them evenly with the rice mixture. Bring 1 pint (550 ml) of the reserved chicken stock to the boil and add it to the pan with the rice and chicken. Cover and cook over a low heat for 20–25 minutes or until the rice is tender and all the liquid is absorbed. Serve in the usual way, or, for a special occasion, place a warm serving dish upside down over the casserole and invert the rice and chicken onto the dish. Serve garnished with segments of orange.

Tunisian Chicken Tagine Pie

Serves 4—6

This Tunisian tagine is prepared in the same manner as a stew, but it is then baked with cheese and eggs to give a firm pielike dish that can be cut into wedges.

4 tablespoons butter or olive oil
1 lb (450 g) chicken, skinned and boned and cut into 1 in (2.5 cm) cubes
2 medium onions, sliced
¼ teaspoon ground ginger
½ teaspoon ground turmeric
½ teaspoon ground cinnamon
¼ teaspoon nutmeg
salt and freshly ground black pepper to taste
6 eggs, lightly beaten
1 cup grated cheese
2 teaspoons dried mint

Melt the butter or oil in a heavy casserole and add the chicken and onions. Brown the chicken on all sides. Add the spices, salt and pepper, stir them into the chicken, and cook for a further 5 minutes. Add enough water to cover the chicken and bring it to the boil. Reduce the heat, cover and simmer for 30 minutes or until the chicken is tender. Pour off the cooking liquid into a pan and reduce it to ¼—½ cup. Transfer the chicken mixture to a baking dish. Preheat the oven to 180°C (350°F, gas mark 4). Cool the reduced liquid and then combine it with the eggs, cheese and mint. Pour this mixture over the chicken in the baking dish and season with salt and pepper. Bake in the preheated oven for 20 minutes or until well set and lightly browned on top. Serve hot cut into wedges.

Chicken and Barley Casserole
Serves 4

A simple English dish, warming and filling on a winter's day.

1 teaspoon dried thyme
2 tablespoons flour
4 chicken joints
3 tablespoons vegetable oil
1¼ pints (700 ml) chicken stock
2 oz (50 g) whole barley
1 clove garlic
2 medium onions, diced
2 medium carrots, sliced
1 medium green pepper, sliced
salt and black pepper to taste

Preheat the oven to 175°C (350°F, gas mark 4). Combine the thyme and flour and dredge the chicken joints in the mixture. Heat 2 tablespoons of oil in a heavy frying pan and fry the chicken joints, turning once or twice, for about 5 minutes or until brown on both sides. Set the chicken pieces aside and pour half the stock into the frying pan. Add the barley and bring to the boil. Lightly boil for 5 minutes. Meanwhile grease a casserole dish with the remaining oil, add the garlic and onions and sauté over a medium heat until they are soft and golden. Add the carrots and green pepper, the barley with stock, and the remaining stock to the casserole dish and season the mixture with salt and black pepper. Add the chicken pieces and cover the dish. Bake for 1 hour. Check the seasoning and serve.

Chicken and Mushrooms Baked in Foil
Serves 4

This simple and elegant Japanese method of cooking chicken really preserves its flavour. It is a low-fat recipe since the chicken is cooked mainly in its own juices. The ingredients include *shiitake*, which are Japanese dried mushrooms. They are available in some oriental food stores; alternatively use large-capped fresh mushrooms.

4 dried shiitake or 4 large fresh mushrooms
1 tablespoon vegetable oil
salt
4 chicken legs (drumstick and thigh) or breasts
4 slices of lemon
3 fl oz (75 ml) soya sauce
3 fl oz (75 ml) lemon juice
2 spring onions, finely sliced, or 1 young leek, finely sliced

Soak the *shiitake* for 20 minutes in warm water. Drain them, cut away the hard stems and criss-cross the caps with shallow knife cuts. Otherwise use fresh mushrooms. Preheat the oven to 190°C (375°F, gas mark 5). Cut four pieces of aluminium foil large enough to wrap each piece of chicken. Brush the dull side of each piece with oil. Sprinkle a little salt on each piece of chicken and each mushroom and arrange a piece of chicken with a mushroom on top on each piece of foil. Top with a lemon slice and wrap securely. Bake in the preheated oven for 35 minutes (check one parcel to see if the chicken is tender). Meanwhile combine the soya sauce and lemon juice and distribute the mixture between four small bowls. Decorate each with a little chopped spring onion or leek. Serve one chicken parcel and one bowl of sauce to each person.

FRUIT
DESSERTS

All the desserts included in this section contain fruit as a main ingredient but that doesn't mean that they are terribly healthy and unsatisfying. I have chosen recipes that are visually appealing and sweet enough to please those of us with a sweet tooth, but which at the same time are not too rich or fatty. There are a few popular dessert dishes with an unusual variation, such as apple pie with cheese in it or meringue pie with a mango flavour rather than lemon. Some of the citrus-fruit-based recipes will double as starters or breakfast dishes. All the recipes are straightforward and, if prepared with fruit in season, economical, but they are also delicious.

Peaches with Fresh Strawberry Sauce

Serves 4

A dessert to be made during those summer months when peaches and strawberries are in season and a punnet of strawberries, almost overripe, can be bought cheaply at the end of the day.

4 large ripe peaches
8 oz (225 g) very ripe strawberries
juice of 1 orange
3 tablespoons Armagnac or other brandy

Skin the peaches by making a small nick in the skin at the stalk end and then plunging the fruit into a bowl of boiling water for 45 seconds. The skin should now slip off easily. Place each peach in a small glass bowl. Wash, hull and drain the strawberries, reserving four firmish ones for garnish. Place the rest in a liquidizer with the orange juice and brandy. Blend unitl the sauce is smooth and fairly thick. This gives a textured sauce and you may prefer to sieve it. Spoon the sauce evenly over the peaches. Chill for 1 hour. Garnish with the sliced reserved strawberries before serving.

Lucky Bag Oranges
Serves 4

Oranges are stuffed with melon, hazelnuts and cream cheese mixed with a little ground ginger. The individual flavours in this unusual mixture of ingredients combine well together in a visually pleasing dish.

4 large oranges
½ small honeydew melon, seeded
1 oz (25 g) hazelnuts, chopped
1–2 tablespoons clear honey
4 oz (100 g) cream cheese (use a low-fat variety if you wish)
¼–½ teaspoon ground ginger

Wipe the oranges and cut off the top third of each one. With a sharp stainless steel knife or a grapefruit knife, carefully cut out all the orange flesh and remove any white pith, keeping the segments as whole as possible. Into a bowl, squeeze the orange juice from the sliced-off orange tops and toss it with the orange segments. With a teaspoon or ball scoop dig out the flesh from the melon and mix it with the oranges. Add the nuts and honey. Cover and chill for 30 minutes. Cream the cheese and ginger together. Fill the empty orange skins with the prepared fruit and small spoonfuls of the cheese mixture.

Grapefruit and Orange Blush
Serves 4

A very simple but delicious starter, dessert or breakfast dish made from grapefruit and orange. Served with a honey and mint sauce.

1 grapefruit
1 large orange
2 tablespoons clear honey
1 tablespoon apple juice
½ teaspoon freshly chopped mint
sprigs of fresh mint to garnish

Wipe the fruit, cut them in half and remove any pips. With a grapefruit knife or a saw-edged stainless-steel knife, cut around the inside of the skin to loosen the flesh from the individual sections and discard the white membrane. Remove alternate grapefruit segments, replacing them with the same number of orange segments and vice versa with the orange. Mix together the honey, apple juice and mint and serve in a side bowl with the fruit. Garnish with mint. Serve either hot or well chilled. To heat, place the filled orange or grapefruit halves under a moderate grill for a few minutes.

Pineapple and Yoghurt Ice

Serves 4

Desserts, such as this one, which can be made in advance and removed from the deep freeze at a moment's notice are most convenient. This recipe also offers a way of making use of a very ripe pineapple which is perhaps not needed immediately.

1 medium-size pineapple
5 oz (150 g) clear honey
1 lb (450 g) thick Greek yoghurt
1–2 tablespoons white rum or Kirsch

Peel the pineapple and remove the central core. Purée half the flesh in a blender and chop the remainder. Place all the pineapple in a saucepan with the honey and bring to the boil. Reduce the heat and simmer for 10 minutes. Cool. Stir in the yoghurt and white rum. Freeze in a shallow freezer-proof dish for 1 hour, then beat until smooth. Refreeze. Remove from the freezer about 10–15 minutes before serving. Serve in scoops in sundae dishes.

Summer Pudding

Serves 4–6

There are only a few weeks in the year when all the soft fruit ingredients of this recipe are in season together but, during this time, it should definitely be on the menu. It is easy to make but looks and tastes splendid. Serve with freshly whipped cream.

6–8 large slices white or brown bread, crusts removed
8 oz (225 g) redcurrants
8 oz (225 g) blackcurrants
8 oz (225 g) granulated sugar
6 tablespoons water
8 oz (225 g) strawberries
8 oz (225 g) raspberries

Put one slice of bread on one side for the top. Use the remainder to line the base and sides of a 2 pint (1 litre) round dish. Put the redcurrants and blackcurrants into a saucepan and add the sugar and water. Bring to the boil and simmer until barely tender, stirring all the time. Add the strawberries and raspberries and cook for 1 minute more. Turn the mixture carefully into the bread-lined dish. Place the extra slice of bread on top and bend over the tops of the bread from the sides towards the centre. Put a saucer on top, pressing down a little until the juice rises to the top. Leave overnight to set. Turn out onto a plate and serve.

Pears Baked in Cream
Serves 4

The calorie-rich but pleasure-giving double cream in this dish is balanced by the goodness of fruit. The pears take only 15 minutes to bake and the preparation of the dish is simple. This trouble-free recipe makes a satisfying dessert.

4 pears, cored, peeled and sliced
1 oz (25 g) unsalted butter
½ pint (275 ml) double cream
2 tablespoons soft brown sugar

Preheat the oven to 180°C (350°F, gas mark 4). Melt the butter gently in a large pan or frying pan and soften the pear slices without browning. Transfer the slices to an ovenproof dish or four individual ramekins and cover them with the cream. Bake in the preheated oven for 15 minutes. Remove, sprinkle the sugar over the top and serve.

Peach and Apple Cheesecake
Serves 4–6

This low-fat recipe may be adapted to use other soft fruit when in season, such as strawberries, raspberries and apricots, or fruits such as mango, cranberries, pineapple, and so on.

4 oz (100 g) oat, muesli or digestive biscuits, crushed
1 oz (25 g) thick honey or muscovado sugar
2 oz (50 g) polyunsaturated margarine, melted
3 large peaches or nectarines
¼ pint (150 ml) low-fat natural yoghurt or thick Greek yoghurt
8 oz (225 g) sieved cottage cheese or curd cheese
1 tablespoon clear honey
2 eggs, separated
¾ oz (20 g) powdered gelatine, dissolved in 5 tablespoons hot apple juice

Lightly grease and line an 8 in (20 cm) loose-bottomed cake tin. Mix the biscuits, honey or sugar and margarine together and, with a damp metal spoon, press the mixture evenly over the base of the tin. Chill. Reserving one peach or nectarine, skin, halve, stone and liquidize the others. Beat the cheese, honey and egg yolks together. Blend the peach purée with the yoghurt and then fold in the cheese mixture. Slowly whisk in the gelatine. In a grease-free bowl whisk the egg whites until stiff. Fold the beaten whites lightly into the peach mixture and pour the lot over the biscuit base. Chill until set. Carefully remove the cheesecake from the tin. Slice the reserved peach and use the slices to decorate the top of the cheesecake.

Banana Fans
Serves 4

Bananas sliced along their length but not cut right through are gently fried in butter or margarine, honey and orange juice, and then served with yoghurt or *crème fraîche*.

4 ripe but firm bananas, peeled
1 oz (25 g) butter or vegetable margarine
juice of 1 orange
1 tablespoon clear honey
thick yoghurt or crème fraîche to taste
ground cinnamon to taste

Slice each banana three times lengthwise to within 1 in (2.5 cm) of one end. Melt the margarine or butter in a frying pan over a low light and add the orange juice and honey. Slightly fan out the bananas and fry each one for 2 to 3 minutes. Turn once during cooking. Serve the bananas on warmed plates with a topping of yoghurt or *crème fraîche* and a sprinkling of cinnamon.

Lancashire Apple Pie
Serves 6

This tangy-flavoured apple pie contains a small amount of Lancashire cheese. It makes an interesting change from the apple pie 'Mum used to make'.

8 oz (225 g) plain flour
pinch salt
4 oz (100 g) butter
2 level teaspoons caster sugar
1 tablespoon custard powder
3 – 4 tablespoons milk
1 lb (450 g) cooking apples, peeled, cored and thinly sliced
1 oz (25 g) sultanas
3 oz (75 g) Lancashire cheese, grated
2 oz (50 g) soft brown sugar
1 tablespoon natural yoghurt
milk or beaten egg

Preheat the oven to 200°C (400°F, gas mark 6). Place the flour and salt in a bowl. Add the butter in pieces and rub it into the flour until the mixture resembles fine breadcrumbs. Stir in the caster sugar and custard powder and add sufficient milk to make a soft dough. Allow to rest in the refrigerator for 30 minutes to 1 hour. Roll out the pastry on a lightly floured worktop and use half to line an 8 in (20.5 cm) pie dish. Mix the apples, sultanas, cheese, brown sugar and yoghurt together and place them in the pie dish. Use the remaining pastry to make a lid for the pie. Seal and flute the edges and make a vent in the top. Brush with milk or egg. Bake for 30 minutes in the preheated oven. Serve hot or cold.

Wensleydale Apple Puff Pastry
Serves 4–6

I come from an area that used to be part of Lancashire and, not wanting to be thought partisan by including only a Lancashire apple pie, here is a cheese and apple pastry from Yorkshire, across the border.

12 oz (350 g) cooking apples, peeled, cored and sliced
2 tablespoons water
3 oz (75 g) Wensleydale cheese, grated
¼ teaspoon cinnamon
1 level tablespoon caster sugar
8 oz (225 g) ready-made puff pastry
milk for brushing
sugar for dredging
sliced dessert apples to decorate (optional)
¼ pint (150 ml) natural yoghurt or cream
juice of ½ lemon for garnish

Preheat the oven to 220°C (425°F, gas mark 7). Put the apples and water in a pan, cover and cook gently until soft and pulpy. Remove from the heat and stir in the cheese, cinnamon and sugar. Leave to cool. Roll out the pastry into a 10 in (25 cm) square and place on a baking tray. Spread the apple mixture over half the pastry and fold the other half over the top. Press down the edges and knock back with the back of a knife to seal. Brush the pastry with milk and sprinkle the dredging sugar over the top. Bake in the preheated oven for about 20 minutes or until golden brown. Decorate with slices of apple dipped in lemon juice to avoid browning. Serve hot or cold with natural yoghurt or cream. If preferred the uncooked pastry can be cut into squares and the apple mixture divided between each to make individual puffs.

Mango Meringue Pie
Serves 4–6

Mangoes are nowadays readily available and can be used to add an exotic flavour to well-known recipes, as with this meringue pie. Buy firm fruits and ripen them at home in a warm place. Use them when they are fully ripe and soft to the touch. The stone in the centre is large and saucer-shaped – to get at the flesh cut lengthwise slices as close to the stone as possible on both sides of the fruit.

8 oz (225 g) shortcrust pastry made according to recipe on p. 17
1 mango, peeled
finely grated juice and rind of ½ lemon
5 oz (125 g) caster sugar
2 eggs, separated

Preheat the oven to 200°C (400°F, gas mark 6). Roll out the pastry and line a 7 in (17.5 cm) flan ring. Bake blind for 15 minutes. Remove the mango flesh from the stone and purée it with the lemon juice. Stir in 1 oz (25 g) sugar and the lemon rind. Beat in the egg yolks, pour the mixture into a pan and heat gently, stirring frequently, until it thickens. Pour the mixture into the flan case. Set the oven to 170°C (325°F, gas mark 3). Whisk the egg whites until stiff, add half the remaining sugar and whisk again. Fold in the rest of the sugar. Pile the meringue on top of the fruit and bake for 20 minutes until golden brown.

Plums in Spiced Custard
Serves 4

The custard in this recipe is made with yoghurt, eggs and honey.

1 lb (450 g) plums, halved and stoned
6 fl oz (175 ml) natural yoghurt
2 tablespoons clear honey
2 large eggs, separated
¼ teaspoon mixed spiced
¼ teaspoon ground cinnamon
2 tablespoons flaked almonds

Preheat the oven to 180°C (350°F, gas mark 4). Put the plums in a single layer in a lightly greased, shallow ovenproof dish. Beat the yoghurt with the honey, egg yolks, mixed spice and cinnamon. Whisk the egg whites until stiff but not dry and fold them into the yoghurt mixture. Spoon this evenly over the plums and sprinkle the top with flaked almonds. Stand the dish in a roasting tin and add enough hot water to come halfway up the sides of the dish. Bake in the preheated oven for 35–40 minutes. Serve hot.

Rhubarb and Ginger Flummery
Serves 4

Rhubarb flavoured with orange is cooked with ginger and honey and then gelatine and whisked egg whites are added and the mixture is chilled so that it sets.

1 lb (450 g) rhubarb, trimmed and chopped
juice and grated rind of ½ medium orange
¼–½ teaspoon ground ginger
3 tablespoons clear honey
2 teaspoons powdered gelatine
2 tablespoons water
2 egg whites

Put the rhubarb into a pan with the orange juice and rind, ginger and honey. Cover and simmer gently, until the rhubarb is quite soft. Dissolve the gelatine in the water and stir it into the rhubarb. Beat the mixture with a wooden spoon until it is smooth. Whisk the egg whites stiff but not dry and fold them thoroughly into the rhubarb when it is semi-set. Spoon the mixture into four individual glasses and chill until set.

Pears in Vermouth and Vanilla
Serves 4

Pears were believed by the Celts to be aphrodisiacs. With the vermouth used in the recipe this dessert could provide a passionate end to a meal. Perhaps it should be reserved for special occasions.

The pears should only just be ripe. Williams pears are recommended.

4 pears, cored, peeled and quartered
juice of 1 lemon
2 in (5 cm) piece of vanilla pod or 1 teaspoon vanilla essence
6 fl oz (175 ml) dry vermouth
1 oz (25 g) granulated sugar

Put the pears in a shallow pan with the lemon juice, vanilla pod or essense and vermouth. Simmer gently for 12–15 minutes. Remove the pears with a slotted spoon and arrange them on a serving dish. Add the sugar to the juice remaining in the pan and boil for 3 minutes. Strain the juice over the pears, cool and then chill before serving.

Cherry Yoghurt Ice Cream
Serves 4

At school I was fascinated by a Charles Lamb essay called 'Ode to a Cherry'. In it he praised the cherry, not for its taste but for the fact that you could spit the stones at your friends. I thought this was a very daring observation for a grown man. This recipe would have provided Charles with both ammunition and a delicious treat for after the battle.

3 eggs, separated
1 tablespoon granulated sugar
6 fl oz (175 ml) natural yoghurt
5 oz (150 g) sweet cherries, stoned and halved
1 tablespoon port or brandy

Whisk together the egg yolks and sugar until they are thick and creamy. Stir in the yoghurt. Whisk the egg whites until stiff but not dry and fold them lightly but thoroughly into the egg yolk mixture. Then fold in the cherries and port or brandy. Pour the mixture into a deep-freeze container about 2 in (5 cm) deep and freeze until solid enough to scoop (about 4–6 hours). Remove the ice cream from the freezer and leave at room temperature for 5 minutes before scooping into serving dishes or glasses.

CONVERSION TABLES
Weights and Measures

Weights

Imperial	Approximate metric equivalent
½ oz	15 g
1 oz	25 g
2 oz	50 g
3 oz	75 g
4 oz	100 g
5 oz	150 g
6 oz	175 g
7 oz	200 g
8 oz	225 g
9 oz	250 g
10 oz	275 g
11 oz	300 g
12 oz	350 g
13 oz	375 g
14 oz	400 g
15 oz	425 g
1 lb	450 g
2 lb	900 g
3 lb	1.4 kg

Exact conversion: 1 oz = 28.35 g

Liquids

Imperial	Approximate metric equivalent
¼ teaspoon	1.25 ml
½ teaspoon	2.5 ml
1 teaspoon	5 ml
2 teaspoons	10 ml
1 tablespoon	15 ml
2 tablespoons	30 ml
3 tablespoons	45 ml
1 fl oz	25 ml
2 fl oz	50 ml
3 fl oz	75 ml
4 fl oz	100 ml
5 fl oz (¼ pint)	150 ml
6 fl oz	175 ml
7 fl oz	200 ml
8 fl oz	225 ml
9 fl oz	250 ml
10 fl oz (½ pint)	275 ml
15 fl oz (¾ pint)	450 ml
20 fl oz (1 pint)	550 ml
1 ¾ pints	1 litre
2 pints	1.1 litres

Oven Temperatures

°F	°C	Gas mark
225	110	¼
250	130	½
275	140	1
300	150	2
325	170	3
350	180	4
375	190	5
400	200	6
425	220	7
450	230	8
475	240	9

British and American Equivalents

This book was written for a British readership. To help the American cook with the system of measurement used, here is a conversion table showing imperial weights with their American cup equivalent.

British	American
8 fl oz	1 cup
½ pint/10 fl oz	1¼ cups
16 fl oz	1 pint
1 pint/20 fl oz	2½ cups
2 pints/40 fl oz	5 cups
2 tablespoons	⅛ cup/1½ tablespoons
8 tablespoons	½ cup
4 oz ground almonds	1 cup
5 oz almonds, unblanched	1 cup
4½ oz dried apricots	1 cup
7 oz aubergines, diced	1 cup
6 oz bamboo shoots, drained and sliced	1 cup
4 oz beancurd, drained	1 cup
6 oz beans (tinned)	1 cup
3 oz beansprouts	1 cup
3½ oz broccoli (fresh), sliced	1 cup
4 oz bulgar wheat	1 cup
4 oz butter	1 stick
8 oz butter	1 cup
4 oz cabbage, shredded, firmly packed	1 cup
4 oz cauliflower, in florets	1 cup
4 oz cheese, grated	1 cup
4 oz cooked chickpeas	1 cup
2 oz flaked, unsweetened coconut	1 cup
3½ oz coriander seeds	1 cup
4 oz sweetcorn kernels	1 cup
6 oz cornflour	1 cup
5 oz courgettes, sliced	1 cup
3½ oz cumin seeds	1 cup
8 oz cooking dates	1 cup
4½ oz wholewheat flour	1 cup
4 oz white flour	1 cup
4 oz green beans, chopped	1 cup
7 oz dried lentils	1 cup
7 oz cooked lentils	1 cup
3½ mangetout	1 cup
9 oz miso (Japanese soya-bean paste)	1 cup
2 oz broken noodles	1 cup
6 oz diced onion	1 cup
2 oz parsley, finely chopped	1 cup
6 oz peanut butter	1 cup
5 oz peanuts	1 cup
3½ oz black peppercorns	1 cup
6 oz tinned pineapple chunks, drained	1 cup
6 oz raisins or sultanas	1 cup
8 oz dry rice (brown or white)	1¼ cups
6 oz sesame seeds	1 cup
8 oz cooked spinach	1¼ cups
1 lb raw spinach	5 cups
6½ oz cooked red beans	1 cup
8 oz granulated sugar	1 cup
6 oz brown sugar	1 cup
9 oz tinned tomatoes	1 cup
8 oz tomatoes	2 medium tomatoes
9 oz tomato paste	1 cup
7 oz vegetable fat	1 cup
4 oz walnuts, chopped	1 cup
6½ oz water chestnuts, drained	1 cup
1 oz yeast	1 cup

INDEX

almonds
    almond and celery soup 32
    peach and wine soup with 26
    toasted: fried celery with 68
anchovy, cheese and potato layers 94
apples
    beetroot and yoghurt salad with 52
    and chicken stir-fry 152
    fondue 95
    lentil-stuffed 80
    mussel soup with 22
    and peach cheesecake 165
    pie, Lancashire 166
    puff pastry, Wensleydale 167
    soup, curried 25
asparagus
    nut cases 63
    with tarragon and walnut sauce 62
aubergine
    bhaji 79
    salad, chilled 48
avocado
    and chicken flan 87
    with hot crab 38
    salad with pink grapefruit 48

banana fans 166
barbecued fish 115–16, 117
barley and chicken casserole 159
basil
    lettuce and cheese roulade with 96
    tomato and tuna tart with 71
batter, beer 120
beans
    butterbean soup 28
    chicken chilli 152
    enchiladas 77
    green bean gratin 64
beansprout salad with celeriac and
    mangetout 47
beetroot
    dip 34
    salad with apple and yoghurt 52
bhajis 78–9
blintzes, chicken 156
bream, baked: chilled with Taratoor
    sauce 130
broccoli
    soup with potato 28
    and tofu stir-fry 60
Brussels sprouts

    and carrot salad 49
    with carrot and cheese sauce 72
bulgar wheat 127
    and fish kibbeh 127
    and lentil stuffing for peppers 74
butterbeans *see* beans

cabbage, white: coleslaw with fruit 46
Caerphilly cheese 82
    Welsh-cheese-and-strawberry-filled
    melon 39
calcium 11
carrots
    carrot and Brussels sprout salad 49
    Brussels sprouts with carrot and cheese
    sauce 72
    spicy carrot soup with orange 30
    carrot soup with potato 27
cashew nuts, stir-fry chicken with 151
cauliflower
    bhaji 78
    curry 65
    Sicilian 38
    and spaghetti carbonade 66
celeriac salad with beansprout and
    mangetout 47
celery
    fried, with toasted almonds 68
    soup with almond 32
Cheddar cheese, English 82
cheese 82–3
    blue cheese dressing 53
    Brussels sprouts with carrot and cheese
    sauce 72
    Caerphilly 82
    and strawberry filling, melon with 39
    Cheddar 82
    cheese, anchovy and potato layers 94
    cheese, pasta and vegetable bake 92
    cheese, potato and onion pie 90
    Cheshire 83
    cottage cheese and crabmeat quiche 89
    and prawn soufflé 134
    tomato soup with 30
    cream cheese and coconut stuffing for
    herring 120
    curd, dip with herbs 35
    Derby 83
    dip 34
    quiche 90
    and spiced fish 93

    dip with walnut and mustard 35
    Double Gloucester 83
    fila pastry fillings 98–9
    flan, courgette and tomato 86
    fondue, apple 95
    goats'; and red mullet in lettuce
    leaves 122
    hard 82–4
    Lancashire 83
    apple pie 166
    leek, cheese and pine nut stuffing 143
    Leicester 83
    and oat burgers 94
    and rice salad, English 55
    roulade, lettuce and basil 96
    tomato and watercress 97
    soft 84
    Stilton 83
    cream cheese, poussins with 91
    Wensleydale 84
    apple puff pastry 167
cheesecake, peach and apple 165
cherries
    and walnut salad 50
    and yoghurt ice cream 170
Cheshire cheese 83
chicken 137–60
    and avocado flan 87
    and barley casserole 159
    blintzes 156
    breasts
    with lime 150
    with mustard 150
    stuffed with leek, cheese and pine
    nuts 143
    bricks 140
    casserole, country 148
    chilli beans 152
    cooking 139–40
    curried roasted 149
    drumsticks baked in chicken sauce 144
    barbecued in foil 144
    filling for peppers 75
    gratin 153
    honey-roasted 148
    kebabs, grilled 146
    and lettuce ball kebabs 145
    microwaving 140
    and mushrooms, baked in foil 144
    parcels in Nori seaweed 42
    pilav, rice and orange 157

pot roast 141
poussins with Stilton cream cheese 91
pressure cooking 140
and rice onepot 142
roasting bags 140
Satay 154
simmered, stuffed with wild rice 147
slow cooking 140
stir-fried 151–2
stock 15
storage 138–9
tagine pie, Tunisian 158
terrine with vegetables and green
    peppercorns 37
thawing 139
wings in garlic and lemon sauce 42
chicory salad with orange 47
chilli
    chicken chilli beans 152
    -hot stir-fry 59
    and tahini sauce, baked in fish with 129
Chinese salad with hot dressing 54
clams 113
cockles 113–14
coconut and cream cheese stuffing for
    herring 120
coleslaw, white cabbage and fruit 46
coley soup with sweetcorn 21
cottage cheese
    and crabmeat quiche 89
    and prawn soufflé 134
    tomato soup with 30
courgettes
    sauce, tagliatelle with 67
    skate with 124
    stuffed 75
    and tomato cheese flan 86
crab 111
    and cottage cheese quiche 89
    hot, with avocado 38
    and shrimp bisque 132
cream, dairy 85
    pears baked in 165
cream cheese and coconut stuffing for
    herring 120
crème fraîche 85
cucumber
    dip 35
    salad, simple 50
    sauce 155
    with sesame ginger dressing 50
    soup with chive 29
curd cheese dip with herbs 35
curry
    apple soup, curried 25
    cauliflower 65
    curried roasted chicken 149
    fish tikka 124
custard, spiced: plums in 168

dairy products 12, 82
    see also cheese; cream; yoghurt
Derby cheese 83
    dip 34
    quiche 90
    and spiced fish 93

dill and orange sauce, poached hake
    with 114
dips
    yoghurt 34–5
    beetroot 34
    cucumber 35
    curd cheese and herb 35
    Derby 34
    walnut, mustard and cheese 35
Double Gloucester cheese 83
dressings
    blue cheese 53
    French 18
    hot 54
    sesame ginger 50

enchiladas, bean 77

fila pastry 17
    cheese-filled 98–9
fish 12, 105–11, 114–31
    baked 109
        in tahini sauce 128
        with hot chilli and tahini sauce 129
    barbecued 115–16
    braised 108
    and bulgar wheat kibbeh 127
    and chips, traditional 119
    cleaning 107
    deep-fried 108
    filleting 107
    grilled 109
    kebabs with marinade 116
    kedgeree 117
    microwaving 109
    and mussel stew, Italian 20
    oily 107
    and pasta 118
    poached 109
    shallow-fried 108
    smoked 110–11
    spiced, with Derby cheese 93
    steamed 110
    stock 16
    in sweet and spicy sauce 125
    tikka 124
    white 107
    see also individual species; shellfish
flans, tarts and quiches 86–90
    avocado and chicken 87
    cheese, courgette and tomato 86
    crabmeat and cottage cheese 89
    Derbyshire 90
    Gower 88
    lettuce and smoked haddock 88
    tomato, fresh 70
    tomato, basil and tuna 71
fondue, apple 95
French dressing 18
fromage frais 85
fruit 161–70
    juice 13
    and white cabbage coleslaw 46

garlic and lemon sauce, chicken wings in 42
ginger
    prawn soup with 23
    and sesame dressing, cucumber with 50

and rhubarb flummery 169
gougères, spinach and mushroom 102
grain 10, 12
grapefruit
    and orange blush 163
    pink, and avocado salad 48
Greek salad 52

haddock
    smoked 110–11
    and cracked wheat salad 55
    kedgeree 117
    and lettuce quiche 88
    soup with sweetcorn 21
hake
    Indian spiced 114
    poached, with orange and dill sauce 114
herring 111
    brochettes 41, 117
    sherry-marinated 40
    soup with vegetable 21
    stuffed with cream cheese and
        coconut 120
    and yoghurt, chilled 121

ice, pineapple and yoghurt 164
ice cream, cherry yoghurt 170
iron 11

kedgeree 117
kibbeh, fish and bulgar wheat 127
kipper pâté 36

Lancashire cheese 83
    apple pie 166
langoustines 111–12
leek, cheese and pine nut stuffing 143
Leicester cheese 83
lemon and garlic sauce, chicken wings in 42
lentils
    and bulgar wheat stuffing for peppers 74
    stuffing for apples 80
lettuce
    basil and cheese roulade with 96
    and chicken ball kebabs 145
    leaves, red mullet and goats' cheese
        in 122
    and prawn sauce, noodles with 66
    and smoked haddock quiche 88
    soufflé 104
    soup with tarragon 31
    and vegetable stir-fry 59
lime, chicken breasts with 150
lobster 111–12

mackerel
    grilled, with hot sauce 126
    Jamaican braised 122
    and rhubarb bake, traditional 123
    smoked mackerel salad 52
mangetout salad with celeriac and
    beansprout 47
mango meringue pie 168
marinade, for fish 116, 118
mayonnaise 15
melon with Welsh-cheese-and-strawberry
    filling 39

meringue pie, mango 168
milk 11, 12
monkfish and pear salad 56
mullet, red, and goats' cheese in lettuce
    leaves 122
mushrooms
    and cheese filling for fila pastry 98
    and chicken baked in foil 160
    Chinese mushroom and watercress stir-
        fry 61
    pâté 36
    and spinach gougères 102
    spinach salad with 44
mussels 112
    and fish stew, Italian 20
    moules à la bordelaise 136
    moules marinière 40
    and pasta 135
    soup with potato and apple 22
mustard, chicken breasts with 150

nettle soup, spring 32
noodles
    Indian summer 69
    with prawn and lettuce sauce 66
nut cases, asparagus 63
nutrition and nutrients 10–11

oat and cheese burgers 94
onion, potato and cheese pie 90
oranges
    and carrot soup, spicy 30
    and chicken pilav 157
    chicory salad with 47
    and dill sauce, poached hake with 114
    and grapefruit blush 163
    lucky bag 163
oysters 112–13
    citrus 132

pasta
    and fish 118
    mussels and 135
    pasta, cheese and vegetable bake 92
    see also noodles; spaghetti, tagliatelle
pastry
    fila 17, 98–9
    wholewheat shortcrust 17
pâté 36–7
    kipper 36
    mushroom 36
    salmon or tuna 37
peaches
    and apple cheesecake 165
    with fresh strawberry sauce 162
    soup with almonds and wine 26
peanut
    butter sauce 155
    sauce, baked chicken drumsticks in 144
pears
    baked in cream 169
    and monkfish salad 56
    in vermouth and vanilla 169
peppers
    red: herring brochettes with 41
    stuffed with chicken 75
        with lentils and bulgar wheat 74

pies
    apple, Lancashire 166
    mango meringue 168
    potato, cheese and onion 90
    Tunisian chicken tagine 158
pineapple
    fresh, with prawns 39
    and yoghurt ice 164
pine nut, leek and cheese stuffing 143
pizza
    sandwich, quick 99
    wholemeal 100
plaice, spiced marinated 118
plums in spiced custard 168
potatoes
    cheese, anchovy and potato layers 94
    chipped 119
    potato, cheese and onion pie 90
    salad with blue cheese dressing 53
    soup with broccoli 28
        with carrot 27
        with mussels 22
    see also sweet potato
poussins 138
    with Stilton cream cheese 91
prawns 113
    and cottage cheese soufflé 134
    with fresh pineapple 39
    and lettuce sauce, noodles with 66
    paper-wrapped 43
    soup with ginger 23
    stir-fry 134
protein 10–11

quiches see flans

rhubarb
    and ginger flummery 169
    and mackerel bake, traditional 123
rice
    and cheese salad, English 55
    and chicken onepot 142
    Chinese brown rice salad 51
    kedgeree 117
    orange and chicken pilav 157
    vegetable and shellfish pilau 131
    wild, simmered chicken stuffed with 147
root vegetable soup, spicy 26
roulade
    lettuce, basil and cheese 96
    tomato, watercress and cheese 97

salads 44–56
    aubergine, chilled 48
    avocado and pink grapefruit 48
    beetroot, apple and yoghurt 52
    brown rice, Chinese 51
    Brussels sprout and apple 49
        and carrot 49
    celeriac, beansprout and mangetout 47
    cheese and rice, English 55
    cherry and walnut 50
    chicory and orange 47
    Chinese, with hot dressing 54
    coleslaw 46
    cracked wheat and smoked haddock 55
    cucumber, simple 50

    with sesame ginger dressing 50
    Greek 52
    monkfish and pear 56
    new potato, with blue cheese dressing 53
    skate and fresh spinach 54
    smoked mackerel 52
    spinach, mushroom and crouton 44
salmon pâté 37
salt 11
sauces
    carrot and cheese 72
    courgette 67
    cucumber 155
    garlic and lemon 42
    hot 126
    hot chilli and tahini 129
    orange and dill 114
    peanut 144
    peanut butter 155
    pizza 100
    prawn and lettuce 66
    strawberry, fresh 162
    sweet and spicy 125
    tahini 128
    Taratoor 130
    tarragon and walnut 62
    tomato 14
scallops 112–13
    stir-fry 133
seaweed, chicken parcels in 42
sesame ginger dressing, cucumber with 50
shellfish 107, 111–14, 131–6
    stir-fry 133–4
    and vegetable brown rice pilau 131
    see also individual species
sherry-marinated herring 40
shortcrust pastry, wholewheat 17
shrimps 113
    and crab bisque 132
skate
    with courgette and capers 124
    and fresh spinach salad 54
smoked haddock see haddock
soufflé
    lettuce 104
    prawn and cottage cheese 134
    sweet potato and walnut 103
soups 19–32
    butterbean 28
    carrot and orange, spicy 30
    celery and almond 32
    chilled 24–6
    crab and shrimp bisque 132
    cucumber and chive 29
    curried apple 25
    fish and mussel stew, Italian 20
    haddock or coley and sweetcorn 21
    herring and vegetable 21
    lettuce and tarragon 31
    mussel, potato and apple with wine
        stock 22
    nettle, spring 32
    peach, almond and wine 26
    potato and broccoli 28
        and carrot 27
    prawn and ginger 23
    root vegetable, spicy 26

tomato, with cottage cheese 30
    with herbs, chilled 24
vegetable, winter 26−9
spaghetti and cauliflower carbonade 66
spinach
    bhaji 78
    and cheese filling for fila pastries 98
    and mushroom gougères 102
    salad with mushroom and croutons 44
    and skate salad 54
sprats, smoked 111
squid 113
starters 33−44
Stilton cheese 83
    cream cheese, poussins with 91
stir-fry
    broccoli and tofu 60
    chicken and apple 152
    chicken and cashew nuts 151
    chilli-hot 59
    prawns 134
    scallops 133
    simple 58
    vegetable and lettuce 59
    watercress and Chinese mushrooms 61
stock
    chicken 15
    fish 16
    vegetable, quick 16
    wine 22
strawberries
    sauce, fresh, peaches with 162
    -and-Welsh-cheese-filling, melon with 39
sugar 11

summer pudding 164
sweetcorn, fish soup with 21
sweet potato and walnut soufflé 103

tagine pie, Tunisian chicken 158
tagliatelle
    with courgette sauce 67
    mussels and pasta 135
tahini
    sauce, baked fish in 128
    and hot chilli sauce, baked fish in 129
tarragon
    lettuce soup with 31
    and walnut sauce, asparagus with 62
tarts see flans
terrine, chicken and vegetable 37
tofu and broccoli stir-fry 60
tomatoes 70
    and courgette cheese flan 86
    sauce 14
    soup with cottage cheese 30
        with herbs, chilled 24
    tart, fresh 70
        with basil and tuna fish 71
    tomato, watercress and cheese roulade 97
tortilla, Spanish vegetable 101
tuna fish
    pâté 37
    tomato, basil and tuna fish tart 71
    and vegetable stuffing for vine leaves 73

vegetable oil 12
vegetables 57−63
    bhajis 78−9

cheese, pasta and vegetable bake 92
    and chicken terrine 37
    Kichiri, Indian 76
    and shellfish brown rice pilau 131
    soup with herring 21
    stir-fried 58−61
    stock, quick 16
    stuffed 73−5
    tortilla, Spanish 101
vermouth, pears in 169
vine leaves, stuffed 73

walnuts
    cherry salad with 50
    mustard and cheese dip with 35
    and sweet potato soufflé 103
    and tarragon sauce, asparagus with 62
watercress
    and Chinese mushroom stir-fry 61
    tomato, watercress and cheese roulade 97
Wensleydale cheese 84
wheat, cracked, and smoked haddock
    salad|55
whelks 113−14
wine
    soup with peach and almonds 26
    stock 22
winkles 113−14

yoghurt 84
    beetroot and apple salad with 52
    and cherry ice cream 170
    dips 34−5
    and herring, chilled 121
    and pineapple ice 164